CULTURE SMART!

ROMANIA

Debbie Stowe

D0951765

·K·U·P·E·R·A·R·D·

This book is available for special discounts for bulk purchases for sales promotions or premiums. Special editions, including personalized covers, excerpts of existing books, and corporate imprints, can be created in large quantities for special needs.

For more information in the USA write to Special Markets/Premium Sales, 1745 Broadway, MD 6–2, New York, NY 10019, or e-mail specialmarkets@randomhouse.com.

In the United Kingdom contact Kuperard publishers at the address below.

ISBN 978 1 85733 452 4

British Library Cataloguing in Publication Data
A CIP catalogue entry for this book is available from the British Library

First published in Great Britain 2008
by Kuperard, an imprint of Bravo Ltd
59 Hutton Grove, London N12 8DS
Tel: +44 (0) 20 8446 2440   Fax: +44 (0) 20 8446 2441
www.culturesmart.co.uk
Inquiries: sales@kuperard.co.uk

Distributed in the United States and Canada
by Random House Distribution Services
1745 Broadway, New York, NY 10019
Tel: +1 (212) 572-2844   Fax: +1 (212) 572-4961
Inquiries: csorders@randomhouse.com

Series Editor Geoffrey Chesler
Design Bobby Birchall

Printed in Malaysia

About the Author

DEBBIE STOWE is a British writer and freelance journalist. She is the author of six travel guides on Eastern Europe and the Indian subcontinent, and several books on the natural world, among other subjects. Her journalism, which appears online and in print in Romanian and international publications such as *The Telegraph* and *Time Out Bucharest*, covers topics including human rights, the environment, entertainment, foreign travel and culture, films, and restaurants. She lives in Bucharest.

The Culture Smart! series is continuing to expand.
For further information and latest titles visit
www.culturesmartguides.com

The publishers would like to thank **CultureSmart!**Consulting for its help in researching and developing the concept for this series.

CultureSmart!Consulting creates tailor-made seminars and consultancy programs to meet a wide range of corporate, public-sector, and individual needs. Whether delivering courses on multicultural team building in the USA, preparing Chinese engineers for a posting in Europe, training call-center staff in India, or raising the awareness of police forces to the needs of diverse ethnic communities, it provides essential, practical, and powerful skills worldwide to an increasingly international workforce.

For details, visit www.culturesmartconsulting.com

CultureSmart!Consulting and **CultureSmart!** guides have both contributed to and featured regularly in the weekly travel program "Fast Track" on BBC World TV.

contents

contents

Map of Romania

introduction

Of all the Eastern European states, Romania probably suffers from the worst reputation, owing mostly to the violent revolution of 1989 and the tragedy of its abandoned children in the 1990s. Move beyond the media images, however, or the clichés of Dracula and creepy Transylvanian castles, and you will discover a fascinating, dynamic country that exerts an inexplicable pull even as it frustrates and bewilders you.

Romania's citizens have retained their "seize the day" mentality despite the deprivations and repression of nearly half a century of Communist mismanagement. While their country rushes zealously to embrace capitalism and conspicuous consumption, they still face the daily problems of a transition economy, which they bear stoically with a shrug and a resigned "This is Romania."

Culture Smart! Romania looks at the ways the past has shaped present-day Romanian attitudes and behavior. We examine the Latin temperament that sees drivers gesticulating and hooting with a fervor that suggests their manhood depends on it. We meet people at home in the grim Communist apartment complexes that they do their best to render cheerful and into which they will welcome you with the very best of what they have. We study them at work—where some stay late into the night determined to forge a better life for themselves, and others play PC solitaire while the boss isn't looking—and at play, partying until dawn in smoky basement dives.

Romanian life is not for the fainthearted. The massive bureaucracy, the occasional curtness, the negative and limiting stereotypes of women and Roma, the appalling poverty, and the risible behavior of the *fițoși*—the ill-mannered nouveau riche—can all be dispiriting. Such drawbacks are more than outweighed by what Romania has to offer, however. High on the plus side is a marvelous sense of "anything goes." Park right across the sidewalk. Smoke wherever you like. Cell phone ringing in a concert? Just answer it. Feeling amorous in the park? No problem. There's little you can do here that will offend.

Romania also offers great business or career opportunities. Expatriate status confers respect and authority. Here, the idea that's been done a dozen times back home is new on the market. Doing difficult things is simple in Romania (it's the simple things that are difficult to do), and Western money goes a long way.

But the biggest draw is the warmth of the people, and the wonderful feeling of being in a place where something is happening. If you can negotiate the pitfalls (and we aim to help you do that), you'll discover a place that will continually surprise and challenge you—difficult, sometimes, to live in, but almost impossible to leave.

Key Facts

Official Name	Romania (România)	Member of the EU since Jan. 1, 2007
Capital City	Bucharest (Bucureşti)	Pop. 1.9 million (approx.)
Main Cities	Arad, Braşov, Cluj, Constanţa, Iaşi, Timişoara	
Area	91,699 square miles (237,500 sq. km)	
Borders	Hungary, Moldova, Ukraine, Bulgaria, Serbia	
Climate	Transitional between temperate and continental, with July the hottest month and January the coldest.	July temperature averages 70°F (21.7°C); January 30°F (1.1°C)
Currency	Leu (meaning lion) = 100 bani	Currency code RON
Population	22,276,056 (est. 2007)	
Ethnic Makeup	Romanian 89.5% Hungarian 6.6% Roma 2.5% others 1.4% (2002 census)	
Language	Romanian is the main language; Magyar is widely spoken in areas with a high concentration of ethnic Hungarians.	English has now taken over from Russian and French as the main foreign language taught in schools.
Religion	Romanian Orthodox 86.7% Roman Catholic 4.7% Protestant 3.7%	Others: Pentecostal, Romanian-Greek Catholic, Muslims, Jews, and atheists

Government	Parliamentary democracy. The head of state is the president, the head of the government the prime minister. The president is elected for a five-year term.	Bicameral parliament consists of the Chamber of Deputies and Senate, both elected every four years under a system of proportional representation.
Romanians Abroad	Diaspora of 8 million people (est. 2006)	They live mostly in the former Soviet states, Spain, Italy, France, and the USA.
Media	Media dominated by television, with state-owned TVR, and private channels ProTV and Antena 1 the most popular. Many viewers have cable TV. More than 100 private radio stations. Many press titles, the majority of which are tabloid or middle market.	The BBC World Service broadcasts on FM in Bucharest and Timişoara. English-language newspapers and magazines (both local and international) are available.
Electricity	220 volts, 50 Hz	Continental sockets and plugs. British appliances require an adaptor, American ones a transformer too.
Video/TV	PAL system	Region 2 DVDs; international TV channels common in hotels and homes
Telephone	Romania's country code is 40	To dial out, dial 00 then country code.
Time Zone	GMT + 2 hours	Romania has daylight saving time.

chapter one

LAND & PEOPLE

GEOGRAPHICAL SNAPSHOT

Variously described as being in Eastern and Southeastern Europe, Romania lies just north of the Balkan Peninsula. It could technically be thought of as being in Central Europe, as it is equidistant between the continent's easternmost and westernmost points, the Ural Mountains and the Atlantic Ocean. It's also halfway between the North Pole and the Equator. At 91,780 square miles (238,391 sq. km), Romania is the fourth-largest country in Central and Eastern Europe. It is bordered by Bulgaria to the south, Serbia to the southwest, Hungary to the northwest, and Ukraine and the Republic of Moldova to the north and northeast. The eastern coast meets the Black Sea. The River Danube runs along the southern border with Bulgaria for just under 670 miles (1,075 km) before turning north and reaching the Black Sea as the Danube Delta. The capital, Bucharest, is 449 miles (723 km) from Belgrade, 398 miles (641 km) from Istanbul, 254 miles (409 km) from Sofia, 526 miles (847 km) from Budapest, and 692 miles (1,114 km) from Vienna.

Romania's terrain is evenly split between mountains, hills, and plains. The countryside reflects a rather ad hoc form of agriculture; orchards and vineyards are often charmingly disorderly. There are green and lush areas flecked with haystacks, bright yellow sunflower fields, and dense forests. The mountains can be snowcapped or verdant depending on the season, not unlike those of Switzerland or Austria. The highest point is Moldoveanu Peak, at 8,346 feet (2,544 meters), in the Southern Carpathians. Natural resources include oil, natural gas, coal, iron ore, nonferrous ore (copper, lead, and zinc), gold and silver ore, sulfur, timber, and salt.

One of the country's most interesting geographical areas is the Danube Delta (Delta Dunării), Europe's largest and best-preserved delta. Now a UNESCO World Heritage Site, it is home to 300 species of birds, 1,200 kinds of plants, and forty-five species of freshwater fish.

CLIMATE AND WEATHER

Romania's position on the edge of the continental landmass gives it elements of both temperate and continental weather. It is also somewhat protected by the Carpathian mountain range, which serves as a barrier to both Atlantic air masses and Russian climatic influences. The climate can certainly be on the extreme side, however; Bucharest summers can see the temperature soar to over 104°F (40°C), while rural winter lows can be as harsh as 14°F (-10°C) or worse, with summers averaging at about 72°F (23°C) and winters 27°F (-3°C). Both of the two main seasons are long, and seem to be encroaching more and more on spring and fall. Even quite young Romanians have noticed a difference compared to when they were children. Seasons can change quite abruptly, although there are still decent periods of very pleasant weather.

In the south, the average annual temperature is 51.8° F (11°C); in the north it's slightly lower at 46.4°F (8°C). Perhaps the best of the weather is in the southeast of the country, where Mediterranean influences bring mild, warm conditions. Rain is not a problem outside the mountain areas—although when it does come it often comes with a vengeance, and the country's substandard drainage systems are overwhelmed. In the cities this seldom results in anything worse than wet socks, but some parts of rural Romania have been severely afflicted by floods in recent years, with deaths reaching the low double figures. Snowfall in winter can be severe.

A BRIEF HISTORY

Romanians put a lot of their contemporary woes down to historical causes, and with good reason. A relatively powerless country—which, its citizens are proud to tell you, has never invaded another state—Romania's location left it at the mercy of great, and often aggressive, neighboring foreign empires. It was rarely left in peace for long enough to develop a sense of its own identity. The Communist regime, as we will see, had the biggest effect, leaving a legacy of bureaucracy, mutual suspicion, and corruption, along with an awe for most things Western.

Prehistory to the Dark Ages

The first traces of human habitation in what is now Romania date back to the Stone Age. Around 10,000 years ago, settled communities relied on hunting, farming, and breeding stock. Estimates vary as to when the Thracians, a group of Indo-European tribes, arrived from the south, but by around 500 BCE they had mixed with the local people to form the Dacians. The Dacians, in turn, split into various tribes, federations, and kingdoms, and under  their greatest king, Burebista, who ruled in the first century BCE, became so powerful that the Romans began to take heed. Julius Caesar decided to wage war against the Dacians but was assassinated before he had the chance—shortly before Burebista met the same fate, slain by his own noblemen. The state was subsequently split into four and then reunified.

Meanwhile, the Roman Empire was growing in might and territory, and the Roman emperor Trajan eventually conquered Dacia in 106 CE. The Romans held on for over a century and a half until successive incursions from the Barbarians prompted them to withdraw, and the brief period of their rule was a significant one for the country; they brought a Latin language and Christianity, as well as advances in farming, mining, commerce, arts, crafts, and culture.

The Dark Ages saw the future Romania governed in succession by the Gothic, Hunnish, Avar, and First Bulgarian empires. Throughout this chopping and changing, the Daco-Romans did their best to continue life in their villages. Their language was developing, as was their religion, under the guidance of the Orthodox Byzantine Empire (the Greek-speaking Roman Empire) at Constantinople.

The Middle Ages and Some Famous Names
By the tenth century the region was divided into small zones, and these eventually merged into three feudal states or principalities—Transylvania, Moldavia, and Wallachia. These are still recognized today, albeit no longer with any administrative relevance. The Magyars of Hungary conquered Transylvania in the eleventh

century, an act that still has ramifications in the present day. It was at this time that the Székely (a Hungarian-speaking ethnic group), the Teutonic Order, and the Saxons were invited by their Hungarian kings to settle in Transylvania. From 1453, however, Moldavia and Wallachia had a new fight on their hands when the Ottoman Turks conquered Constantinople. While the Ottomans expanded their empire through the annexation of much of Hungary and the Balkans, the Romanian principalities held out, with their princes heading the Christian resistance for several hundred years.

Most legendary among these princes—for very different reasons—were Stephen the Great and Vlad the Impaler. The latter, Vlad Țepeș in Romanian, ruled Wallachia three times: in 1448, from 1456 to 1462, and again in 1476. His notoriety stems from the cruel tortures he inflicted on a variety of victims, from local peasants, women, and children to ambassadors, merchants, and invading Ottomans. From the most infamous one, death by impalement, he derived his appellation. A Romanian story suggests that under Țepeș it was possible to leave a bag of gold in the street, where it would remain untouched, so great was the fear of punishment. There were also rumors—which historians do not credit—of cannibalism, which led to Țepeș' inclusion in the Dracula myth of Bram Stoker's novel. Despite his sadism, however, in Romania Ţepeş is remembered chiefly for his justice and spirited defense against the Ottomans, whom he successfully held at bay for some time.

Vlad the Impaler's contemporary, Stephen III of Moldavia, or Stephen the Great (Ştefan Cel Mare), is remembered for different reasons. Throughout

his long reign (1457–1504), he fortified Moldavia, preserved his state from Hungarian, Polish, and Ottoman attempts to conquer it, and won thirty-four out of thirty-six battles he waged. One of these was a historical first, a Christian victory over the Ottomans that led Pope Sixtus IV to pronounce him *verus christianae fidei athleta,* or "True Champion of Christian Faith." Aside from the cultural

development that took place during his reign, his legacy includes the many self-built churches and monasteries that today are UNESCO World Heritage Sites. In 2006, 40,000 viewers voted him the greatest Romanian of all time in a poll organized by a Romanian TV channel.

Despite the efforts of Vlad the Impaler and Stephen the Great, the Romanian principalities could not hold the Ottomans at bay indefinitely without help from the West and were obliged to recognize Turkish suzerainty. They were never occupied, however, and unlike much of Byzantium, Serbia, Bulgaria, and Hungary, never became provinces or had Turkish governors, instead paying a tribute to the Turks for the privilege of retaining their autonomy. At this time the Romanian states were the protectors of Christianity for the entire Orthodox East.

The Beginnings of Modern Romania

The defeat of the Ottomans did not put an end to foreign intervention in Romania. In 1699 the Treaty of Karlowitz gave Transylvania to Habsburg Austria. The Austrians in their turn began to expand their empire. They co-opted Oltenia, part of Wallachia, in 1718, and held on to it for almost two decades. This was followed by the Habsburg seizure of Bucovina in northwest Moldavia in 1775, and the Russians also got in on the game by occupying Basarabia, the eastern half of Moldavia, in 1812. Indeed, the period was marked by the growing political influence of the Russian Empire, a power that would come to dominate the Romanian political landscape until the late twentieth century.

Meanwhile, the late eighteenth century had seen the emergence of a Romanian bourgeoisie whose sense of shared identity prompted it to call for the union of the three states into an independent country. The wave of liberal national revolutions that swept through Europe in 1848 reached Romania with popular democratic uprisings in the three principalities. The first phase of the union—the merging of Moldavia and Wallachia—was achieved in 1859, following Russia's defeat in the Crimean War. At the time, the new entity was ruled by the elected Prince Alexandru Ioan Cuza, but seven years later a combination of scandal and political opposition forced him to abdicate, and he was succeeded by the German Prince Carol (Karl) I of the house of Hohenzollern-Sigmaringen.

Trouble with the Turks simmered on. In 1877–78, Romania fought with Russia against the Ottomans. Its contribution was considered instrumental, and the country was recognized as an independent state in the 1878 Treaty of Berlin, making it the first independent national state in Eastern Europe. It became a kingdom three years later, with Carol I as king. This did not address the issue of Transylvania, however, which by then had become part of Hungary, despite the protestations of the 70 percent of its inhabitants who were Romanian. The period also saw early emigration from Romania to the USA and Canada in search of economic opportunities and freedom from political oppression. Surrounded by three huge empires, Romania turned westward for guidance in its cultural, educational, military, and administrative development; it developed a particular affinity with France, eventually joining the Western Allies during the First World War in 1916.

The World Wars and In Between

Romania's aim in declaring war on Austro-Hungary was to win back Transylvania, and this was accomplished at the end of the war, along with the inclusion of various minorities living in the region. Its campaign, however, was less than illustrious. Two-thirds of the country, including Bucharest, were occupied by the Central Powers of Germany, Austro-Hungary, the Ottoman Empire, and Bulgaria, and in 1918 it was obliged to negotiate a peace treaty with Germany, although it did rejoin the war five months later.

The period that followed the end of hostilities is fondly remembered in Romania today. The country had almost doubled its size and population. Great or Greater Romania (*România Mare*) saw the different regions officially united; a modern-day political party even uses the phrase as its name to recall the pride of that era. Some of the country's most beautiful buildings, typically designed by foreign architects, date from this time, earning Bucharest the appellation "the Paris of the East." There were economic and cultural advances, a relatively functional democracy, and some press freedom during this period, but it was not to last.

For two decades after the end of the war, the country was a liberal constitutional monarchy, but tension was developing around its minorities. The 28 percent of the Romanian population that was made up of Magyars (ethnic Hungarians),

Germans, Jews, Ukrainians, and Bulgarians, among others, sought representation, and several political parties giving voice to them sprang up. Unfortunately, nationalistic and anti-Semitic parties were also gaining in popularity. One, the Iron Guard, won 15.5 percent of the vote in the 1937 general elections.

Carol II, having renounced the throne in 1925, returned from exile in Paris in 1930 to supplant his son Mihai (Michael) as king. He soon began to feel the pressure of the rise of fascism, and the following year joined many countries in continental Europe by establishing a dictatorship. With public disenchantment with the political parties running high, and violence commonly used to end political arguments, there was little opposition to Carol's decision to abolish Parliament. Already scandalizing even the most ardent royalists with his licentious private life, he banned all other political parties and began to rule the country with help from a disreputable coterie of personal advisers, many of whom were introduced to him by his mistress Elena Lupescu.

Unsurprisingly, things did not go well. In 1940 Romania lost territory to the USSR (through occupation) and Hungary (through the Vienna Dictate) without a shot being fired. Carol II was forced to abdicate in favor of his son, Mihai, but power was effectively taken over by General Ion Antonescu with the help of the Iron Guard, which he later suppressed. Antonescu became military dictator, leaving Mihai king in name alone.

In 1941 Romania entered the Second World War under the command of the German Wehrmacht in order to get back its territories from the USSR, and was awarded Transnistria by Germany.

In 1944 a pro-Allied coup by King Mihai resulted in the arrest of Antonescu and the placing of Romanian forces under Red Army control, after which they sustained heavy losses fighting the Nazis in Hungary and Czechoslovakia. After the war the Paris Peace Treaty saw northern Transylvania, which had been annexed by Hungary, returned to Romania, but the northern territory lost to the USSR was not recovered and went on to become the Republic of Moldova. The 1945 Yalta Agreement between the leaders of the victorious Allies— Franklin D. Roosevelt, Winston Churchill, and Joseph Stalin—saw Romania, along with the rest of Eastern Europe, allotted to the Soviet "sphere of influence," marking the start of Romania's shift to Communism.

Communism

The Russian occupation of Romania at the end of the Second World War saw the abdication and exile of King Mihai and the establishment of a Communist People's Republic in 1947. Soviet economic methods were adopted, farming was collectivized, properties were seized by the state, and traditional Romanian culture was altered or obliterated. The country's first Communist leader was former tramway worker Gheorghe Gheorghiu-Dej. Initially an ardent Stalinist—his anti-Semitic campaign coincided with Stalin's own Jewish purges—he toed the line of Stalin's successor, Nikita Khrushchev, after the death of the Russian dictator in 1953. Khrushchev advocated peaceful coexistence with the West, and subsequently withdrew Soviet troops from Romania. When Gheorghiu-Dej became the president of the country in 1961, however, he turned his back on Soviet policy, a stance that won him favor in the West, and began a campaign of industrialization. In later years, before he died in 1965, he opened diplomatic relations with the West, including the USA.

Following Gheorghiu-Dej's death, the helm of the country passed to Nicolae Ceaușescu, a former shoemaker's apprentice and hitherto low-profile figure who had joined the Communist Party as early as 1932, when it was still an illegal organization. During a jail term in 1943 for his antifascist activities, Ceaușescu had shared a cell with Gheorghiu-Dej; he went on to become his protégé, rising steadily up the party rankings. He continued his predecessor's assertion of Romanian independence from Soviet influence, denouncing Russia's invasion of Czechoslovakia in 1968. This won him fans among both his public and Western leaders; he was awarded the

THE HOLOCAUST IN ROMANIA

Anti-Semitism, which had grown in the nineteenth century, played a big part in public and political discourse with the rise of right-wing, nationalistic parties in the interwar period. Jews were barred from professional associations, forbidden to marry Christians, and some were required to reapply for citizenship. Eighty anti-Jewish laws were passed in two years at the start of the 1940s, and the Iron Guard began a campaign of violence and looting against Jews. In 1941 over 10,000 Jews were killed in the Iaşi pogrom.

The persecution continued after the fall of the Iron Guard, when the Antonescu regime allied itself with Nazi Germany. Deportations did stop in 1943, when Antonescu began to seek peace with the Allies, but he continued to oppress the remaining Jews with forced labor and heavy taxes. It was not until 2003 that Romania set up the Wiesel Commission to investigate and educate the public about the country's role in the Holocaust. Its report assessed the number of dead as between 280,000 and 380,000. The commission was set up as the result of international outcry after top Romanian politicians, including President Iliescu, denied that a Holocaust had taken place in Romania. Only now is it being studied and commemorated in the country.

Danish Order of the Elephant and an honorary Knight Grand Cross of the Order of the Bath, a British order of chivalry, although both were later rescinded. Life in Romania was less repressive in the early days of Ceauşescu's rule, although the Securitate, the country's brutal secret police, were fully functioning, contraception and abortion were banned, and the childless were heavily taxed to encourage population growth.

Ceauşescu's Personality Cult

It was following Ceauşescu's visit to China, North Korea, and Vietnam in 1971 that the political situation in Romania worsened considerably. Ceauşescu was tremendously impressed with the hard-line version of Communism that he saw in Asia, and upon his

return he set about replicating it at home. He expanded the power and reach of the party, and increased censorship, propaganda, and the indoctrination of young people. He also began to build up a personality cult, indulging himself—and his wife, Elena, who played an increasingly important role—with grand public pageants. As his lifestyle grew ever more lavish, the Romanian people were sinking into miserable deprivation. The economic growth built on the back of foreign loans had turned to grinding poverty. Long lines for scarce meat, bread, and fruit were commonplace, and food was rationed, as were electricity, heating, and gas. Although the Gheorghiu-Dej policy of industrialization had been kept, little of what was produced was of high enough quality to be sold abroad. Meanwhile, the Securitate had practically made Romania a police state.

The disastrous urban planning concept of systematization, the mass rehousing policy introduced in 1974, saw large areas razed and rural people resettled in towns. Churches, monasteries, and homes were demolished to make way for poorly funded "prestige" projects that often did not reach completion. The monotonous, substandard apartment complexes that were erected as part of the systematization drive still scar Romania's cities and towns. The centerpiece of the policy was the Palace of the People (*Casa Poporului*), a giant administrative building that remains one of the biggest in the world. Work began in 1984 and, although the building is in use, it is still not finished.

By 1989, Communist regimes were falling across Eastern Europe, leaving Ceaușescu increasingly isolated. Prompted by government attempts to evict a Hungarian clergyman who had criticized the regime in the international press, a protest broke out in the western city of Timișoara among the pastor's parishioners. They were soon joined by passers-by, many of whom were religious Romanian students who believed the eviction was another attempt to restrict religious freedom. Over the following days the protest grew and intensified. The army was sent in, and dozens of protesters were shot. The government dispatched workers from the neighboring region of Oltenia to suppress the demonstrations, but instead they joined the protesters.

On December 21, the state organized a mass rally in Bucharest to condemn the Timișoara uprising. Ceaușescu was in the middle of a speech from the balcony of the Central Committee building when bangs were heard, which were attributed to the Securitate firing on the crowd. The people, initially afraid, started to jeer at the Communist leader; after attempts to quell the dissent failed, Ceaușescu and his wife fled inside the building, from where they attempted to escape by helicopter. Meanwhile, the Bucharest protesters began to celebrate and riot.

Government forces fired on the people. Hundreds died from bullets and stab wounds, or were crushed by tanks. Fire trucks turned water jets on the public, while the police beat and arrested people. Eventually, and for unclear reasons, the security forces switched sides to fight alongside the demonstrators. The tide had turned. In all, more than 1,000 people died in the week of protests. The Ceaușescus were arrested by the army, put on "trial" for genocide against their own people by a self-designated extraordinary military tribunal, and shot on

Christmas Day. Many of the facts surrounding
the revolution remain unclear, and rumors of
foreign instigation persist.

After Communism

The joy that followed the fall of the Ceauşescus
was short-lived. Rather than power going to
someone untainted by the old regime, the figure
who emerged as the new leader was Ion Iliescu, a
Communist Party official who had been seen as a
threat and sidelined by Ceauşescu. Within hours
of the dictator's overthrow, Iliescu was on TV,
hailing the revolution. Even before the old leader
was shot, he seized control of the country with
other party members as the leader of the National
Salvation Front (FSN), which became the
provisional ruling authority. The sudden converts
to democracy repealed some of the most
unpopular Communist laws and ran as candidates
in the May, 1990, elections where—thanks to the
FSN's stranglehold on the media—they were
overwhelming winners. The new government was
packed with former Communist officials, who
tried to persist with a socialist agenda.

Horrified by the direction their new
"democracy" was taking, Bucharest protesters
again took to the streets. Iliescu denounced the
demonstrators, led by students and university
professors, as "hooligans," and called in the
miners to quash the protests. In the infamous
"Mineriad" of June 1990, the workers set about
clubbing the protesters, killing more than a

hundred people, according to NGO estimates, and wounding another thousand. Iliescu later thanked the miners for stopping "the fascist attempt to create a coup d'état." A year later the miners were back in the capital calling for higher wages, and this eventually brought down the government.

Throughout the 1990s, Romania struggled to shake off the Communist legacy. The economy shrank and inflation was rampant, sometimes higher than 300 percent. Poverty was, if anything, initially worse. Things did not start to improve until the former Communists lost power in the general elections of 1996 following the start of media liberalization, which loosened the state's grip on the news, and a better organized opposition. Major reforms were then implemented. Iliescu managed to hang on to the presidency, twice winning reelection, and remained on the scene until as late as 2004.

Iliescu first returned to office in 1992, following the drawing up of a constitution—over which the government was accused of fraud. His support base consisted of rural people and industrial workers fed propaganda by the state-controlled TV channel, the only station available to them at the time. In 1996, with his media monopoly gone, Iliescu lost the presidency to Emil Constantinescu of the center-right Democratic Convention. In 1997 a comprehensive economic reform package was announced and the Securitate files were opened, but the difficulty of establishing a workable coalition meant that with the exception of a few critical reforms, the government found it hard to get its decisions enacted. Consequently, Iliescu returned to power in 2000, after victory over the far-right candidate Corneliu Vadim Tudor. His prime minister was Adrian Năstase, who was repeatedly accused of wrongdoing, including corruption, bribery, money laundering, trafficking influence, and censorship. At the time of writing, several cases involving Năstase are ongoing.

Looking West

The year 2004 promised to herald a new era for Romania. Iliescu departed from politics, barred by the constitution from seeking a third term (it was decided that his first tenure did not count toward the total of two). In a vote that attracted the usual accusations of electoral fraud, the presidential candidate from his Social Democrat Party (PSD), Năstase, was defeated by the charismatic mayor of Bucharest, Traian Băsescu, a former ship's captain. On top of that, Romania was accepted into NATO. This did not spell the end of political upheaval, however. Relations between Băsescu and his prime minister, Calin Popescu-Tariceanu, soon deteriorated, and the president was temporarily suspended, pending a referendum on his impeachment—a vote that, as one of the country's most popular politicians, he duly won. Meanwhile, figures with links to the Securitate still hold top political positions.

Ultimately, however, most Romanians agree that whatever the faults of the current regime, it is preferable to anything they have had before. The country's EU accession, on January 1, 2007, has been a great boost to its economy and self-image, and as new generations of Romanians less shaped by the old regime come to take their place in society, there is genuine hope that living standards will continue to rise and the country will finally shake off its Communist legacy.

GOVERNMENT

Romania's constitution dates from 1991, although it was amended in 2003. The document establishes the country as a democracy and market economy, and enshrines the values of human dignity, civic rights and freedoms, the unhindered development of the individual, justice, and political pluralism. It obliges the state to implement free trade, protect competition, and provide a favorable framework for production. It also establishes the structure of the government, providing for a president, a parliament, a constitutional court, and a separate system of civil and criminal courts that includes a supreme court.

A democratic republic, Romania's system of government is semi-presidential—president and prime minister share executive functions and both participate in day-to-day state administration. The president, who is the head of state, is voted in by the public, and his (or her) official residence is Cotroceni Palace in Bucharest. The presidential tenure was increased from four to five years by constitutional amendment in 2003, and the president can hold office for up to two terms. His duties include safeguarding the constitution, overseeing foreign affairs, and ensuring the proper functioning of public authorities. He is also supreme commander of the armed forces and chairman of the Supreme Defense Council, and can mediate between state powers as well as between the government and the public.

The prime minister, based at Victoria Palace, Bucharest, is the head of government and picks the members of his or her cabinet, which is subject to a parliamentary vote of approval. Typically the prime minister is the head of the ruling party or coalition, but if no party has a majority, he is appointed by the president.

Parliament is bicameral, with a Senate (*Senat*) of 137 members and a Chamber of Deputies (*Camera Deputaților*) with 332. Both chambers hold elections every four years. Elected officials are selected on the basis of party lists through proportional representation, with the

exception of the president and mayors. The voting age is eighteen, and there is universal suffrage.

The country is divided into forty-one administrative counties (*judeti*), plus the capital, Bucharest, each of which is run by an elected county council and mayor, with a prefect appointed by the government who is responsible for public services and central agencies at the local level. The prefect can block a local authority action if he or she considers it illegal or unconstitutional; the matter is then referred to an administrative court. Local councils are responsible for spending the budgets they receive from the state.

POLITICS

Romania's transitional and turbulent post-Communist political landscape has seen some significant changes in its party lineup. Currently, the main parties are as follows: the Democratic Party (PD), a center-right group associated with President Traian Băsescu; the National Liberal Party (PNL), a centrist party led by current prime minister Călin Popescu-Tăriceanu, whose governing coalition with the PD has now broken down; the PSD, now in opposition, formed by Communist Party members following the revolution; the Conservative Party, a minority party headed by Dan Voiculescu, a high-ranking Securitate collaborator who has been investigated for corruption and money laundering; the Hungarian Democratic Union of Romania

(UDMR), an alliance that represents ethnic Hungarians; and the Greater Romania Party (PRM), a strongly nationalist organization.

Personalities have long overshadowed policies and principles in Romanian politics, and alliances are regularly forged across supposed ideological divides. In the 2004 elections, the PD was able to abandon its coalition with the left-leaning PSD and join up with the center-right Justice and Truth Alliance. Perhaps this focus on people explains why Romanian politics is characterized by a such a large number of highly personal attacks. In the run-up to elections prominent public figures have been widely accused of many things, including homosexuality, rape, corruption, and collaboration with the Securitate.

Elections also routinely come with allegations of fraud and censorship. In 2004, there were accusations that the incumbent PSD bussed supporters to four different districts, where they were alleged to have voted four times. In the same campaign, half of the copies of satirical newspaper *Academia Caṭavencu* were removed from newsstands early on publication morning when the title ran a critical article on PSD candidate Adrian Nãstase.

The suspension of President Traian Bãsescu in April 2007, which the Romanian people voted against in a referendum, came amid a long-running period of infighting between Bãsescu and his prime minister Cãlin Popescu-Tãriceanu. Each has accused the other of lying, and Băsescu even phoned in to a TV talk show to criticize the prime minister on air. The upshot of all this is that elections routinely suffer from low turnouts and Parliament is the second-least trusted institution in Romanian public life, slightly above the unions, according to a 2005 Gallup poll.

THE ECONOMY

The Romanian economy has been through something of a roller-coaster ride since the collapse of Communism. In 1989 it was in a dire state, with an obsolete industrial base, and it continued to decline until 1993. A major problem was repayment of debt to the West. Ceaușescu had run up huge arrears in building up state-owned industry in the 1970s. Determined to be free of foreign creditors, he ordered all efforts to go into repaying the debts, leaving his own people with little to sustain them and the economy in tatters. Things got worse before they got better, with the economy shrinking through much of the 1990s. The government implemented an ambitious program of structural reforms in the areas of energy-intensive industries (see below), agriculture, the financial sector, and macroeconomic stabilization.

Garment and shoe manufacturing, metal, the extracting and processing of primary goods (timber, marble, rock), food processing, oil

UNIONS

Despite a long tradition, under Communism trade unions were centralized and their role shrank to the transmission of party policy to the common man. Following the revolution, unions, or syndicates, at first proliferated, with the result that they were competing for members with unrealistic promises, thus undermining their efficacy and bargaining power. With workers' rights and the economy in general so precarious, however, the unions served a real need, and in the early 1990s they began to involve themselves more in politics, with the establishment of a political party based on union membership.

Today their significance is greatly reduced, owing to resistance to unionization by employers (including foreign investors), less demand from workers and lower membership, and some unions' failure to adopt modern methods; however, in some fields, particularly heavy industry, membership remains relatively high, and unions were instrumental in improving pay and protecting workers in the large privatizations of the 1990s.

refining, and chemical derivatives are the main industries in Romania, followed by pharmaceuticals, heavy machinery, and household electronics. A high percentage of people—estimates range from around 35 to 45 percent—are still employed in agriculture,

much of it subsistence farming. The remainder
are divided between industry and services, with
slightly more in the latter category.
Unemployment has been steadily falling, and
currently stands at around 5 percent.

STUCK IN THE MIDDLE

Romanians tend to blame many of their historical
and current woes on their country's location.
Wedged between the Russian, Ottoman, and
Austro-Hungarian empires, the country was
subject to repeated invasions and buffeted
between various foreign powers. Many believe
that, given this history, no country could have
emerged unscathed. Some Romanians feel bitter
that their country was delivered into the Soviet
sphere of influence at the end of the Second
World War, and think that if it had been located
further west, things would have been much better.

Influences from both East and West are evident
in today's Romania. Many of the country's young
people are very Westernized. They learn English
and other Western European languages with
enthusiasm and dedication, consume largely
Western (particularly American) media in the
form of music and films, dress like their
European peers, and long for their country to
continue its assimilation and appropriation of EU
standards. On the other hand some, mainly older,
Romanians hark back to the Soviet era and its
values. They bemoan the licentiousness that they

perceive as a Western disease, which they see in homosexuality, drugs, and sexual freedom. A subgroup, the Roma community, betrays Eastern influences. Many Roma women dress in traditional Indian-style costumes, while the men favor Syrian- and Turkish-influenced suits and shoes with pointed toes.

A PERIOD OF TRANSITION

It is difficult for an outsider to imagine how bad life was in Communist Romania less than two decades ago. Emerging from this dark period, and with the prospect of EU membership giving an added impetus to reform, the country has been changing at breakneck speed. The pace of this change is visible in the cityscapes, which often seem to resemble large building sites. Businesses spring up and close down frequently. Fluctuating wages, currency exchange rates, and macroeconomic indicators have all been unpredictable.

The transition period has also had a notable effect on the country's value system. After nearly half a century of censorship, Romania was suddenly exposed to news, views, and— perhaps most obviously—products and commercialism from the outside world. Romanians were suddenly forced to question much of what they had believed in for decades. This is perhaps one reason why some unfounded opinions (especially about the West) and superstitions remain. Other effects of the sudden arrival of capitalism include a general susceptibility to big business and advertising; having had no exposure to commercials, Romanians have not developed the savvy of the Western consumer. Meanwhile, the sudden acquisition of riches has led to the formation of a Romanian nouveau riche, a moneyed class trying to behave like an elite.

BUCHAREST

The early history of Bucharest is as up and down as the story of Romania itself, with advances followed by periods of decline from the time of

the Roman Empire until it became the capital toward the end of the nineteenth century. The provenance of its name is uncertain, but one suggestion is that the settlement was founded by a shepherd called Bucur. Burned down by the Ottomans and abandoned by the Romanian princes in the early seventeenth century, Bucharest was rebuilt and prospered, despite being afflicted by a plague, a devastating fire, and various occupations over the next two hundred years. Even then, the social division between rich and poor was pronounced. Officially chosen as the capital in 1881 when the Kingdom of Romania was established, Bucharest's population grew rapidly, while cultural and architectural advances earned it the moniker "the Paris of the East" or "Little Paris."

During the Second World War Bucharest suffered bombardment by both the Allies and the Luftwaffe. The Communism that was established at the end of the war changed the face of the city, with grim, monotonous apartment blocks built to house Ceaușescu's workers as part of the process of systematization, and large parts of the old town razed to make way for the Communist civic center and the grandiose People's Palace. A massive earthquake in 1977, measuring 7.4 on the Richter Scale, also brought down many old buildings. The turbulent period from 1989 included the riots and demonstrations of the Romanian Revolution, further protests at the hijacking of power by the supposedly ousted Communists, and the brutal 1990 "Mineriad." The city continues to be subject to upheaval, now in the form of the many urban regeneration projects intended to bring its housing, facilities, and infrastructure up to twenty-first-century Western standards. It is now brightened by designer boutiques and capitalist trappings that would have made its Communist rulers wince.

Today Bucharest is by far the most important city in the country in terms of size and economics. With a population of just over 1.9 million, it is the sixth-largest capital in the European Union, bisected by the Dâmbovița River. The Municipality of Bucharest, as it is administratively known, is divided into six sectors, each of which has its own mayor. The city does not have as many instantly recognizable landmarks as some other capitals. Its most distinctive edifice is the People's Palace, or Parliament Palace (*Palatul Parlamentului*) as it is now officially known. While there is some pride that the country has

(nearly) completed such a big construction project, most Bucharest inhabitants prefer the Athenaeum, a neoclassical concert hall in the center of the city. The Athenaeum is no more than a few hundred meters from the former Central Committee building, from where Ceaușescu delivered his final address, which is now part of the Senate.

Many Romanians find their capital very distinctive from the rest of their country. Like most big metropolises, it is busier, dirtier, and has a faster pace of life than elsewhere. Romanians from outside the city also consider Bucharest people rude, a claim that there is some evidence to support; a *Reader's Digest* survey in 2006 found Bucharest the second-rudest city out of thirty-five tested from around the world.

THE COUNTRYSIDE

In order to understand the "real Romania" one should head for the countryside. While residents of the main cities enjoy rising wages, increasing prosperity, and decent shops and restaurants, the rural areas show how far Romania still has to go. Although around half the population lives in the countryside, these areas are still poorly supplied with essential goods and services. Many people live without running water, relying on outside latrines and wells. The horse and cart is a common means of transport. Many villages are without a doctor, there are few banks, and shops have only the most basic provisions. Subsistence farming supports many families, unemployment is high, and salaries are low even by Romanian standards. A project is now under way to bring basic communication equipment—public phones, fax machines, and computers—to villages in the form of subsidized telecenters, but as yet it has only had a limited rollout.

Despite this deprivation, the Romanian countryside is in some respects the backbone of the national culture. Costume, cuisine, and folk music all developed from rural traditions. Because of migration to the cities—both voluntary, economic migration and the forced displacement that took place under Communism—a large percentage of the urban population are either from the countryside or are the children of rural people, and some pastoral customs continue to be observed in towns.

VALUES &
ATTITUDES

At first sight, particularly in the cities, Romania might seem to differ little from Western democracies. People spend time with family and friends, are notionally if not devoutly religious, and enjoy shopping, sports, and socializing. Further interaction with local people reveals significant quirks in the Romanian psyche, however. Although many people are now city dwellers, a large number of young Romanians have parents and grandparents from the country, and rural ideas and customs dominate the culture. This is particularly evident in the superstitions to which many people cling. Religion is another factor informing views and attitudes. The result is that despite the provocative dress of many Romanian women—even some professional ones—and the armies of semi-naked models in newspapers and magazines and on billboards, attitudes toward sexual matters remain largely traditional. The other big influence is, of course, Communism. To cover the many ways in which the old regime has left its mark on modern-day mores would require a whole book in itself. A suspicion born of years of living among unknown

Securitate informers, the suppression of civic spirit, and a weary acceptance of suffering are among the main consequences, along with a slavish obedience to authority figures. The Communist legacy is at odds with young Romanians' eager embrace of all things identified as Western, creating the tension that characterizes a society in transition. Despite all the social upheaval, some things, such as the warm Romanian hospitality, have remained constant.

ORPHANS, DOGS, AND DRACULA

Romanians have a keen awareness of the stereotyping that they are convinced clouds all foreigners' perceptions of them. They fear that their country is perceived from abroad as the sum of a few pejorative clichés: orphans, stray dogs, and Dracula. Although Romanian child care has progressed significantly since haunting images of disturbed children in institutions were broadcast across the Western world in the early 1990s, the subsequent lack of media interest in reporting improvements means that many foreigners retain the association. Stray dogs are indeed a serious problem, or at least a nuisance. The Dracula associations, meanwhile, seem to have developed out of stories of the brutal Vlad Țepeș, which are thought to have inspired Irish writer Bram Stoker's novel *Dracula*. Few Romanians had heard of the Dracula myth before 1989, and were initially bemused when tourists began arriving in

Transylvania clutching books about the count and expecting sinister Gothic castles. Bran Castle near Brașov, which has now become a sort of unofficial Dracula's castle—on the strength of Țepeș having reportedly spent a couple of days in the dungeon—is in fact a rather pretty building, offering little in the way of macabre thrills.

By contrast, the things and people that many Romanians expect to be famous outside their borders seldom are. It is only recently that the average Romanian has had any prospect of traveling abroad, and there has therefore been a certain ignorance about the outside world and an inability to gauge Romania's place in it (the result largely of Communist censorship and propaganda, both of which stoked nationalism). It's quite common to have conversations with Romanians who are surprised that you've never heard of a particular musician or athlete, or are unaware of a certain fact about the country that everybody there knows.

PATRIOTISM AND ANTI-PATRIOTISM
Romanians generally divide into two camps: the fervently patriotic and the cynical. Age, level of

education, and experience of foreign travel tend to affect the position that someone takes. Anyone who grew up and was educated under the Communist regime was repeatedly told how wonderful their country was, and that they were lucky to be experiencing a "golden age." Although the poverty and deprivation were pretty much undeniable, in the atmosphere of paranoia created by the legions of Securitate informers, this was not something about which people could talk openly. There was no source of objective news from the outside world, and rumors that the Western world was decadent, crime-stricken, and drug-ravaged gained currency. This was possible partly because there were few people (aside from the Communist higher-ups themselves) who had been elsewhere and could therefore deny the rumors, and also because the idea had a psychological advantage: Romanians had no hope of going to live in the West, so it was more comforting to believe that life there was as bad, in its own way, as life at home.

Although information about the world is now available to anyone who is inclined to look for it, comforting ideas about the greatness of Romania have been harder to budge—particularly among the older generation. Some still hark back to the Communist era as a golden one, citing the former high levels of employment, low crime rate, and lack of drugs to back up their case.

In the other corner is the cynical younger generation. Many of the anti-patriots did not spend enough time in the Communist education system for the brainwashing to be irreversible. They are typically fluent in English, among other languages, and keen students of life outside the state borders. Sickened by the corruption and deprivation that have hindered progress, they tend to assume the worst of their homeland and often react to the latest political or business scandal with a weary shrug. Typically well educated, many are keen to travel abroad and sometimes feel embarrassed to be identified as Romanian, believing this leads foreigners to make certain negative assumptions about them. They have a wry motto about their homeland: "Romania's a nice country—shame it's populated."

Whether they esteem their country highly or not, the majority of Romanians care about what happens to it. Those who leave tend to do so as a last resort; many young, educated people feel a responsibility to stay and use their skills and values to make things better. This is usually the option favored over going abroad, and many who do go abroad fully intend to return after making enough money to secure themselves a decent life here. This view is seldom presented in the tabloid press of Western Europe, which assumes that people from Romania are desperate to get out and settle in the West for good. Some are and do, but many others see their stay abroad as a short sojourn before returning to a better life back home.

THE LATIN TEMPERAMENT

Romania is a Latin country culturally. People are typically demonstrative, talking loudly and emphasizing the point they are trying to make with dramatic gestures. Many are quickly moved to emotion, which is conveyed through raising both the volume and the pitch of the voice—it's not uncommon for men to end up exchanging squeaks if they get into an argument. To an outsider, many conversations between Romanians appear to be altercations. Often these are straightforward discussions, but delivered with what seems like fury. If a Romanian addresses you in a blunt or animated way, do not assume he is angry with you—it is more likely that this is his normal demeanor. Conversations come with frequent interruptions, and if two people are talking at the same time, there is no guarantee that one will feel obliged to stop. Don't feel offended when people interrupt, as they are not being deliberately rude—in the flurry that is a Romanian conversation, sometimes interrupting is the only way to be heard.

This said, the hot Latin temper is also in evidence. Romanians can be quickly moved to anger, although often this is about show and not losing face rather than a serious intent to follow through; it is rare to see anyone actually coming to blows. In terms of public behavior, many Romanians are uninhibited. There is no embargo on public displays of affection, and amorous couples can assume quite intimate positions in public, particularly in parks, with no sense of impropriety. The Latin *joie de vivre* also comes out when people let their hair down. Nightclubs and parties are usually vibrant affairs, often going on late into the night. Rarely will you see a miserable Romanian sitting down in a nightclub, complaining about the music or DJ.

Owing to shortages and periods of social upheaval, Romanians have not been able to develop the famous style and elegance associated with other Latin countries in Europe, such as the Italians—with whom they most closely identify—and the French. They do exhibit proclivities in this direction, however, and many spend a lot of time, money, and effort on their physical appearance. Another aspect of this fixation can be seen in offices: rather than sticking up photos of friends and family around their work desks, many people will instead put up a favorite picture of themselves.

Romanians are a warm and tactile people. Their general friendliness and openness mean that they find some foreigners, particularly Northern Europeans, standoffish and cold by comparison. Do not be surprised if you consider yourself an affable person and a Romanian judges you as distant; they are merely applying the standards of their own society. People here are quick to extend the hand of friendship and cannot understand why some other nationalities don't do the same. Romanians are particularly friendly to foreigners, and like them to form a good impression of their country. They are sometimes more reticent with compatriots, and foreign visitors occasionally find that people who have been enormously warm and welcoming to them can be slightly cooler if introduced to a Romanian partner or friend. (See below for a further exploration of this mistrust.)

Although many Romanians, particularly well-educated ones, do settle in the USA, Canada, and the UK, in general emigrants have a preference for Italy and Spain, countries where they feel more familiar with the language and behavior of the people. You will notice a marked difference in the demographic spread of Romanians traveling between Bucharest and Rome, and those going between Bucharest and London, for example.

THE AFTERMATH OF COMMUNISM

Although it has been nearly two decades since Communism officially ended in Romania, the country's near half-century under the totalitarian regime has left an indelible impression on almost all aspects of life. Because the state was ubiquitous, influencing home as well as public life, traces of Communist thinking are evident in the most personal issues, and are very difficult for some Romanians—particularly the older generation—to shake off. Many quirks of local beliefs and behavior can be traced back, at least in part, to the socialist period.

No dissent or questioning of the system was permitted under Communism, and this has instilled a conformity of thought and acceptance of authority that makes Romania fertile ground for religious leaders and advertising companies. Because Romanians have never learned the questioning process, long-held beliefs and prejudices are difficult to shift. The education system featured—and still does, to an extent—learning by rote over encouraging creativity and independent thought. Many people can fire off the names of capital cities with ease, but if asked to give their own opinion on something, they will founder. Conformity is still highly prized, and individuality is viewed with suspicion. Even something as innocuous as wearing slightly unusual clothes will attract strange looks. Another legacy is the poor standard of living conditions, services, and products, all accepted as normal. Summer regularly sees the hot water turned off in parts of Bucharest, and water, gas, and power outages punctuate the whole year. Few residents see this as anything out of the ordinary or reason for complaint.

CUTTING CORNERS

Most Romanians grew up under a corrupt system, and trying to outsmart it in little ways has become a way of life. Some people are quite ambivalent about dishonesty. There is even a word to describe unscrupulous behavior that earns a degree of admiration because of the élan with which it is executed: *şmecherie*. Cheating, cutting corners, and petty pilfering are not met with the same disapproval as in Western society.

One cause is corruption in the education system in the early days of Communism, where struggling, or lazy, students could buy good grades through gifts to the (very underpaid) teacher, while able students who were unable or unwilling to do so were given poorer marks. This practice had the effect of severing the link between merit and actual grades, to the extent that for many education was about doing what had to be done to attain the grades rather than learning and improving as a person. Many people have carried this mentality into their adult lives and even try to cheat on tests that go toward serious qualifications. This is not so prevalent now, but some teachers remain open to bribery, and parents may hire their child's teacher for extra lessons out of school hours both to help the child improve and to incur the teacher's favor.

This tolerance of cheating is evident in other aspects of life, such as the widespread practice of fare evasion. It often appears incongruous that a moral, decent, sometimes religious Romanian will be quite blasé about such matters. It is important to remember that for decades, Romanians have seen the dishonest, greedy, and crooked—the șmecheri—rise in power and wealth in their society, while honest folk remain mired in poverty. Until the country becomes more meritocratic, a process that is already underway, the habit of dishonesty is likely to stay.

CONSPICUOUS CONSUMPTION

In some ways, Romanians are still in the process
of celebrating their release from Communism and
rebelling against its values. One of the most
visible signs of this is the embrace of conspicuous
consumption. This is quite understandable: for
many years the country suffered great
deprivation, denied the technological and
aesthetic luxuries enjoyed by the West. In the
years after the revolution, new and advanced
products found their way onto the local market.
Anything perceived as Western—symbolizing the
opposite of everything the Romanian people had
endured for so long—was pounced on, as
Romanians enjoyed their first taste of capitalism
and freedom (which became closely linked).
Salaries were still not high, but with many young
Romanians still living at home and therefore
having few expenses, people were happy to
splurge large portions of their salaries on securing
the latest "must-have" (a term that has been co-
opted into the Romanian language).

Conspicuous consumption is most visible in a
few main areas. The first is cell phones. Many
Romanians have two, even three, phones.
Sometimes one is a work phone and the other a
personal one, but there is also an element of just
enjoying the technology and status derived from
owning the latest gadget. Men often wear their
phones on a cord around their necks, proudly
displaying the newest model. There is also a huge
appetite for downloaded ring tones: a mobile

phone belonging to anyone under forty is
far more likely to blast out the latest song
by the American rapper of the moment
than to emit the standard buzzing or
bleeping. While many foreigners are
content to use their phone until it
gets lost, stolen, or broken, young
Romanians tend to upgrade as soon
as they can afford to. It is therefore important not
to make snap judgments about someone's wealth
based on the normal indicators, like the gadgets
that they might have. Owning a €500 cell phone
does not imply that someone has a €2,000 salary;
it's quite possible they have a €250 monthly
salary and spent two paychecks on their phone.

Unsurprisingly, designer labels are also highly
popular. The logos (or copies of varying quality)
of Calvin Klein, Versace, Hugo Boss, Armani,
and Prada are common sights, and a sizable
proportion of young Romanian men are partially
or entirely clad in Nike. While EU pressure has
led to the government taking trademark and
copyright infringements more seriously, fake
copies are still common, and counterfeit
merchandise is even on sale from apparently
respectable businesses. A similar trend is visible
in cosmetics: some Romanians talk earnestly
about the latest fragrance from Calvin Klein or
Dior. Aside from the low salaries, the country is a
dream market for the beauty industry, as some
young people tend to splash on large amounts of
fragrance, and women apply cosmetics liberally.

Conspicuous consumption is largely the preserve of those from Bucharest and the other large cities; elsewhere there is too much real poverty for people to be able to indulge in gadget mania, and the media is also too restricted for rural Romanians to know what the latest must-have is, even if they don't have other priorities for their money. Even in smaller towns and villages, however, people will often own odd items that seem way out of proportion with their general income level—a household will spend heavily on its TV set, for example, while its home furnishings remain modest.

Seeing the love of labels and must-have mobile handsets, some people reach the conclusion that Romanian society is shallow and materialistic. This is overly harsh, however; the country is still in transition, and after years of poverty and restriction, most Romanians are simply enjoying the pleasures—dressing up and owning nice things—that Westerners take for granted. Unencumbered by Western middle-class notions that showing off material possessions is vulgar, Romanians are relieved no longer to be so poor—and they're not embarrassed about showing it.

ATTITUDES TOWARD ETHNIC MINORITIES

Hearing amiable, educated Romanians airing their views on the local Roma population is likely to be one of the first-time foreign visitor's biggest culture shocks. A plainspoken people with no concept of political correctness, some Romanians may casually drop into the conversation such comments as, "I hate gypsies." Before denouncing them as irredeemable racists, however, it's important to try and understand the background of the tensions involved.

The Roma are a distinct racial group within the country, and while there is some integration, it remains limited. To the ethnic Romanian's mind, much of the crime in the country is committed by gypsies, who control illegal activities such as drug trafficking, burglary, and prostitution, have a stranglehold on other, legal businesses such as flower selling, and indulge in price-fixing and other failures to respect business ethics. Many Romanians believe that the police allow gypsies to get away with things for which the authorities would come down hard on an ethnic Romanian. They also attribute much of the crime committed in Europe by Romanians to gypsies, and believe that foreigners see no difference between the two, which leads them to the conclusion that Roma are responsible for Romania's bad reputation abroad and the stigmatization that honest, hardworking Romanians face when they try to build a life elsewhere. Of course, many people realize that part of what might drive a gypsy to crime is lack of opportunities in the legitimate labor market—

a result of the widespread discrimination they suffer—and that a vicious circle is in place. An aggravating factor is that most Romanians in the major towns are forced by the substandard Communist-era housing complexes to live in close proximity to each other. The typically social and communal Roma lifestyle does not go down well with neighbors living on the other side of a thin wall, and this ratchets up the enmity.

Some Romanians are also prone to make the odd disparaging remark about people from Turkey and the Middle East, which they call the Orient, and although it is rare, you may even hear people use the word "nigger" with little idea of how offensive it sounds. Black and Asian visitors to Romania will certainly attract stares, and groups of young people may engage in silly behavior such as shouting "Jackie Chan" when they see someone who looks Chinese. All of this comes not from malice, but from the scarcity of people of a different ethnicity in the country, and lack of education about them. As Bucharest's business community becomes increasingly international, people of different skin color are becoming a more common sight, but in the smaller towns and villages the appearance of such a foreigner would be something of an event.

A useful comparison is the situation in the UK fifty years ago; lack of exposure, education, and awareness, rather than hatred, lie behind most racist-sounding comments. The Romanians' overriding impulse is often to welcome strangers to their country and home, and being of a different color is no barrier to making friends and being accepted into local groups—indeed, the perceived glamour of the exotic can even help.

ATTITUDES TOWARD WESTERNERS

Westerners—particularly white ones—will have an entirely differently experience. Whatever their view of the world outside Romania, most people love to make friends with foreigners from the West. This seems to stem both from a desire to practice their language skills and to "access" the West by asking you about your home country and comparing your values and opinions to their own. As a foreigner, you'll get special dispensation in many different areas. Locals will refrain from much of the stronger criticism and bluntness they dish out to each other. Your opinion will be listened to and taken seriously. People will go all out to make a good impression. Some Romanians are slightly in awe of foreigners, whom they believe to be rich, sophisticated, and powerful.

This perceived wealth and status is a particular draw for many young women. It is fairly common for a male expatriate of advancing years (and often waistline) to form a relationship with a much younger, attractive local woman. It is tempting to write this off as exploitation or gold digging, but that would be to ignore all of the factors involved. The majority of young women in Romania have grown up in at least semi-poverty, with little hope of going abroad— something that has only become an option for most in recent years. Not only does an expatriate boyfriend open up an exciting world of sophistication (restaurants, foreign travel, culture), but he may also be more modern and less chauvinistic than his Romanian peers.

Ultimately, whether as a partner, a friend, a business colleague, or a stranger in the street, Romanians almost always go out of their way to make you feel welcome, valued, and at home.

ATTITUDES TOWARD AUTHORITY

A very oppressive state has instilled in Romanians a strong obedience to authority. Under Communism, any rebellion was brutally clamped down on, and people have got used to doing what they are told. Even figures with a very small amount of power—such as the administrators of old apartment complexes—can run a regime of fear, and will be very surprised if you do not comply with their every demand.

Latter-day sources of authority include big corporations. Having had no exposure to advertising for decades under Communism, Romanians have not developed the skepticism required to question the impressive-sounding claims of advertisers and marketers. If it's on TV, some seem to think, it must be true. Other authority figures are foreigners, who are often assumed to have superior knowledge and status, regardless of whether this is borne out in reality.

THE STATE VERSUS THE INDIVIDUAL

Perhaps the best example of the past attitude of the *nomenclatura* of the Romanian state is the People's Palace, the huge monstrosity built by Ceauşescu, second in size only to the Pentagon. Visible from almost all over the city, it looks down imposingly, dwarfing the individual as if to say, "We are the state." In the post-Communist period the state has become far more benign, but certain aspects of official behavior suggest its representatives still see themselves as authority figures first and public servants second. Examples of this attitude include the surly and self-important demeanor of many civil servants and public officials, as well as the way state bigwigs get around the city: a dramatic cavalcade comes speeding along, with traffic police stationed at points along the route, preventing other cars and pedestrians from blocking the way. A man with a megaphone will bellow, "Stay on the right!", obliging all motorists to pull over so the politician can glide through unimpeded. The frequency of this type of incident in Bucharest means that this is not a privilege reserved for the few top people, but routinely extended to lesser politicians. These same politicians are the ones in charge of allocating money to projects to ease the city's congestion— congestion they rarely, if ever, experience.

PRIVACY AND PERSONAL SPACE

The hugely intrusive Communist state that controlled almost every facet of people's personal lives has largely eroded the concept of privacy. Neighbors take a prurient interest in each other's business and do not always wait to be invited before entering someone else's home if they have an issue to resolve, such as a problem with a leaking pipe. Don't be surprised if new acquaintances ask you some very direct questions about your salary, belief in God, marital status or intentions in this respect, or opinions on gypsies, homosexuality, and other issues that might be conversational no-go areas in your home country. Again, this is not seen as prying or intended to make you feel uncomfortable—people just consider these legitimate discussion topics, and if they are curious about something, they will ask.

Personal space in Romania is also much less valued than you may be used to, and often does not really exist as an idea at all. Waiting in line was a big part of Communist life here, and unless one guarded one's position someone else was liable to cut in, so older people have a tendency to stand very close to the person in front of them when waiting in line. The Latin ease of physical contact and closeness means that in cinemas, restaurants, and all forms of public transportation, other people are likely to sit much closer to you—regardless of how many other free tables or seats there are—than you are used to. This is not necessarily an attempt to be rude or intimidating;

many Romanians simply do not recognize the importance of personal space to others. After all, if the seat or table is free, why shouldn't they sit there? It is important to be aware of this, particularly if you are a woman; if you're sitting alone in an empty metro car and a man sits directly opposite you, this is not the potentially threatening situation it could be at home.

Perhaps the most obvious manifestation of the lack of regard for privacy is the staring you might experience. Many Romanians are in the habit of staring at anything or anyone they perceive as slightly different or interesting. Because this is the norm, there is no taboo on looking at someone, and if you eventually catch the person's eye they will feel under no obligation to then avert their gaze, as would probably happen elsewhere. Nor are Romanians in the habit of breaking into a smile if there is prolonged eye contact. This can seem, to someone unused to it, to be an act of intimidation or hostility. It is seldom meant as such, and is merely curiosity. As a foreigner, your dress and demeanor will mark you out as unusual and you are likely to attract a few stares, but this is something visitors get used to if they stay for any length of time.

TALL POPPY SYNDROME

Although its values are shifting irreversibly westward, Romania still has a collectivist culture more reminiscent of the East than of Western individualism. Membership of the group—be it family, friends, or workmates—is usually expected to take priority over one's individual wants and needs. On top of that, the predominantly working-class culture of the cities brought by the rural dwellers moved en masse by Ceaușescu emphasizes community solidarity over self-betterment. The result is that anyone who seeks to improve themselves (aside from by getting richer, which everyone understands) can sometimes meet resistance. Lifestyle improvements such as jogging or quitting smoking or drinking seem to baffle many people, who perhaps construe such desires in others as a rejection of their values. Romanian society also has an element of *Schadenfreude*, summed up by the saying, "I wish my neighbor's goat would die." The flip side of all of this is the strong solidarity of local communities.

MEN AND WOMEN

Gender roles in Romania are more rigid than the visitor might be used to. Very few women are solely homemakers—hardly any families could afford this—but apart from the most modern couples, the vast majority of domestic and child-rearing duties are performed by the woman. There are strict ideas about ideal masculine traits—strength, dominance, being a good provider—and feminine traits—being submissive, gentle, and sexually attractive—and people who contravene the norm may meet resistance and disapproval. In more traditional, working-class Romanian families it is accepted that the husband is the boss, and some men may address their wives in abrupt tones that might surprise a foreigner. Women, particularly older ones, may be quite submissive to their husbands.

Domestic violence remains a problem in Romania, where the prevailing attitude is that a woman becomes her husband's property when she marries him, and beating one's wife is considered normal by many. Surveys suggest that around one in five women has been physically abused by a partner. There have, however, been attempts to change attitudes in recent years, such as the Law on Preventing and Combating Domestic Violence adopted in 2003, and an initiative announced in 2005 to get bridegrooms to attend a three-day course to deter them from beating their wives, although the takeup of this has not yet become widespread.

Outside the home, many men (both the young and urbane, and older, traditional individuals brought up in Romania's more chivalrous recent past) will often allow a woman to pass through a door first. Restaurant bills are automatically presented to the man, and male waiters will help a woman on with her coat.

While women make up much of the workforce, the low-skilled jobs that they traditionally hold are more poorly paid than low-skilled men's jobs. Few women have made it into the higher echelons of Romanian business and politics.

Part of this is due to the entrenched view that a woman's chief value is in her physical appearance. The presentation of women in the media continues to be sexist—something the EU has criticized—and semi-naked women appear on everything from the sports pages to bottles of antiseptic. This has seeped into the Romanian mentality, and many men cannot understand why a woman would not be flattered to be stared at and commented on as she passes on the street; indeed, some local woman do seem to welcome and encourage this kind of attention.

Many Romanians, particularly the better educated ones, find the feminine ideal held up in their country extremely frustrating. Because feminism was largely discredited by its association with Communism, however, the voices arguing for women's rights in Romania today are faint and few. As a foreigner, you are likely to be spared much of the worst discrimination; nationality seems to trump gender in Romanian perceptions. However, anyone who values gender equality is likely to find many aspects of gender associations in local life and culture frustrating and backward.

Attitudes to sexual activity before marriage are changing in line with the rest of Europe. The ideal among the older generation remains to wait until one is married before having sex; the majority of younger people are far more in tune with the permissive values espoused by MTV and the West than they are with traditional notions of chastity, however, and few but the most devout or naive parents would expect their children to be virgins on their wedding night.

SUSPICION

It is estimated that the Communists had a network of 400,000 to 700,000 informers, equating to between 2 and 4 percent of the population. This frightening statistic (at this rate, there were likely to be several living in any given block of apartments) made suspicion a necessary self-defense mechanism for the average Romanian. This is perhaps one reason why many Romanians do not extend the same warm and open welcome to their compatriots that they do to foreigners, and people are liable to assume the worst of others.

Suspicion has also contributed to the country's nepotism: people are often more willing to enter into a relationship, either business or personal, with someone to whom they are connected in some way (a relative or a friend of a friend) than a complete stranger. Expatriates and visitors often notice that local people who have been enormously helpful and friendly to them may clam up when a fellow Romanian is involved.

PASSIVITY AND FATALISM

Romanians were pretty much powerless during their four decades of Communist rule. The regime crushed civic spirit, and even now that freedom of speech has theoretically been restored, people are used to bearing their misfortunes and deprivations stoically and not protesting or complaining via the channels provided. Political demonstrations are rare, and are usually small affairs over niche concerns. Given the traditionally incompetent and corrupt authorities, it is easy to understand why many people despair of achieving real change, and save their energy. The phrase "*Asta e,*" meaning "That's the way it is," sums up this feeling of impotence and resignation.

The Little Ewe

This tendency toward fatalism is summed up in the story of *Miorița* (The Little Ewe), one of Romania's most enduring pastoral tales. The ewe tells her young master that two of his fellow shepherds are planning to murder him and split his assets. Instead of escaping or outwitting his would-be assailants, as a Western story would surely demand, the shepherd accepts his fate and instead sets about planning his funeral. Romanian writers and thinkers have presented various interpretations of the story, but few foreigners can view the shepherd's attitude as anything other than unfathomably pessimistic.

HOSPITALITY

It is hard to think of more generous hosts than
Romanians. No matter how poor the people
welcoming you into their home are, they will give
you the very best of what they have. Out will
come the best meat, and more food and drink than
you could ever manage to consume. Neither your
plate nor your glass will remain empty for long,
as seconds and thirds are proffered regardless of
whether you're still hungry or thirsty. It is often
difficult to refuse another extra serving from an
enthusiastic host, and it's better to accept
graciously if possible.

If you're eating out, the host—usually the most
senior man of the party—will foot the bill,
regardless of protestations. This can be awkward,
as the most senior man is not always the highest
earner, and the foreign visitor may feel it unfair
for him to cover the expenses of a group night
out. A foreigner is unlikely to be allowed to play
host, however—the locals will consider it their
duty to treat you—so there's little that can be
done about it without offending someone's pride.

MONEY

Unlike in some parts of the Western world, there
is nothing embarrassing or vulgar about money in
Romania. The only restrictions on discussing
salaries come from company bosses who do not
wish to have disgruntled employees on their
hands; it is not considered vulgar or intrusive to

ask someone's salary or reveal one's own. In a restaurant, local people may debate how much to tip directly in front of the waitstaff—which can be mortifying for any foreigners present—and then tell the staff what to take for themselves, rather than surreptitiously leaving the money on the table and exiting.

Many Romanians take pride in owning and showing off expensive things, and people are far more likely to spend their money on items that others will see, such as clothes, cars, and gadgets; a Romanian driving a top-of-the-line foreign car often drives home to a relatively modest apartment, and someone who drinks an expensive imported beer in a club will go home and drink the cheapest local brand.  This attitude is perhaps best summed up by toilet paper. Because many people are not used to entertaining in the home, the bathroom will seldom be used by outsiders. Although luxury brands are available, the two common types of paper are both very rough and cheap. Such a poor-quality product would not even reach the market in many other countries, but someone who uses the cheapest brand may well have a state-of-the-art TV and expensive car.

Social class and money are tightly correlated. When local people speak of the "middle class," they are not referring to someone who is well educated or has certain refined tastes and values—

they mean someone earning a good income. A millionaire will be considered to be of a high social class no matter how boorish his tastes and behavior. Romanian reverence for money may seem crass, but having been deprived of it for so long, people enjoy what money they have without shame.

RELIGION

Although Romania is officially a secular state, the vast majority of people—86.7 percent—consider themselves members of the Romanian Orthodox Church, according to the 2002 census. The remainder are Roman Catholics (4.7 percent), Protestants (3.7 percent), members of various Pentecostal denominations (1.5 percent), and of the Romanian-Greek Catholic Church (0.9 percent). There are also a few Muslims, Jews, and atheists. Many Romanians simultaneously interpret the Bible literally and accept the theory of evolution without seeing any inconsistency— there has never been a significant public debate about evolution here.

Religious symbols are common: families often have icons in their homes, and many taxi drivers hang crosses over their rearview mirrors. Whether this denotes great piety is another matter. Although a high proportion of Romanians will cross themselves when they pass a church, actual church attendance is far lower, with a 2006 survey suggesting that 26 percent of Romanians go at least once a week. Celebrations such as Easter and

Christmas do draw bigger congregations. Religion is not considered a taboo subject, and you may be questioned about your position. Faced by someone of another religion, a Romanian would be likely to listen politely to that person's beliefs, but privately consider them misguided or bizarre.

The Communist regime did its best to marginalize religion, bulldozing churches and synagogues. Today religion is under threat not

from the state, but from the European trend toward secularism; as in other countries, younger Romanians are less devout than their parents, and urban dwellers less so than rural communities.

SUPERSTITION

Alongside religion, several other strong beliefs have a hold on Romanian life in the form of superstition. This is much stronger in the countryside, where people are less educated and their lives more dependent on the whim of nature, so anything they can do to encourage good luck, they will. Spilling salt on the table is considered unlucky, but this can be offset if the spiller puts some of it on their forehead. Salt is sometimes

thrown in the middle of a storm to try to end it.
Dropping certain things (cutlery, matches) heralds
an auspicious visit or good luck. Brides should not
see each other in church—because weddings are
concentrated around certain times of the year for
religious reasons, there may be many ceremonies on
the same day—and siblings should not marry in the
same year. A bouquet of flowers given as a present
should consist of an odd number; an even number is
the norm for funerals.

One of the superstitions most likely to impact on
you is the phobia of moving air, known as *curent*.
Many Romanians believe that fans, air-conditioning,
and drafts are harmful, responsible for every ailment
from cold and toothache to meningitis. They cannot
bear to sit in a room with both the window and the
door open, and would rather endure sweltering heat.
This can be immensely frustrating if you share a hot
office with local colleagues. Unfortunately, logic-
based attempts to convince anyone that moving air
is safe and pleasant seldom work, and other
explanations for maladies (such as attributing
toothache to poor dental hygiene) are usually
dismissed. Even occasional articles in the press by
doctors and dentists assuring readers that moving
air is not the cause of hordes of maladies fail to dent
the belief. The standard hospitable deference to a
foreigner's wishes may persuade your host to leave
the window open and allow you a bit of a breeze on
a hot day, but the fear is so entrenched that it is
usually not long until someone rushes over to close
it to stop the draft in a panic.

chapter three

CUSTOMS & TRADITIONS

Owing to their propensity for collective behavior, customs and traditions are important to Romanians. During the bleak years of Communism, public holidays, birthdays, and weddings were among the rare occasions when people could relax and enjoy themselves, and they are celebrated with much revelry and fanfare. People tend to stick to tried and trusted ways of passing holidays and celebrating events. Alcohol often features significantly.

PUBLIC HOLIDAYS

Public holidays are much looked forward to in Romania, with discussions and plans about what to do starting several weeks in advance. Because people tend to stick to traditional activities and timeworn customs, you can expect certain places to be very busy on public holidays, namely parks (providing the weather is good) and resorts (coastal in warm weather, mountains throughout the year). Forms of civic entertainment, such as free concerts, are frequently organized around these days. Beer

PUBLIC HOLIDAYS

January 1 and 2
New Year (*Anul nou*)

Moveable
Orthodox Easter Sunday and Monday (*Paştele*)

May 1
Labor Day (*Ziua muncii*)

December 1
National or Union Day (*Ziua naţională* or *Ziua unirii*), celebrating the union of Transylvania with the Kingdom of Romania in 1918, the foundation of the modern state. It is commemorated with a large military parade attended by political leaders, speeches, and the switching on of the Christmas lights.

December 24
Christmas Eve (*Ajunul Crăciunului*)

December 25 and 26
Christmas (*Crăciun*)

OTHER OFFICIAL HOLIDAYS AND OBSERVANCES

March 1
First day of spring (*Mărţişor*)

March 8
International Women's Day (*Ziua internaţională a femeii*)

Moveable
Heroes' Day or Ascension (*Ziua Eroilor* or *Înălţarea*), the 40th day after Easter. Changed to May 9 by the Communists in 1948, the link between Heroes' Day and Easter was restored in line with stipulations in the Treaty of Versailles.

June 26
Flag Day (*Ziua Tricolorului*)

December 6
Constitution Day (*Ziua Constituţiei*), when the referendum on the Romanian Constitution was held in 1991.

often plays a big role here, and later in the day the atmosphere around such gatherings is not always pleasant.

If public holidays fall midweek, the day off is often shifted to make a long weekend. This is done to avoid disrupting the workweek, either by the state or by companies themselves.

FAMILY OCCASIONS
Christmas
Romanian Christmas celebrations are not dissimilar to festivities in Western countries. Things do get started a little earlier, on St. Nicholas's Day on December 6 (Santa Claus is known as *Moş Crăciun*, or Old Man Christmas); on this day, children's boots, which have been polished and left out the night before, are traditionally filled with small presents, and sometimes a stick to warn the little ones to behave well for the year ahead. In the run-up to the day itself, carols (*colinde*) are sung at schools and offices, and many places celebrate with a party.

The real traditions are observed in the villages, however. Pork is the customary Christmas meat. Villagers normally buy a pig, if they don't already have one, and slit its throat in their backyard before dismembering it for meat. Whatever is edible is eaten over the Christmas period, including the skin (*şoric*), which is lightly toasted and eaten then and there. EU legislation has now outlawed the throat slitting, however, and from now on the animal will have to be dispatched by electrocution, shooting, or tranquillizers, under the monitoring of a local inspector. The pork meat lasts throughout the holiday and is served up in different forms, including *sarmale* (cabbage leaves stuffed with rice, pork, and vegetables), with city dwellers often getting their share from relatives in the country.

Many people attend church on Christmas Eve, which is also the time when they put up and decorate the tree. As in many countries, the next day is a family affair, consisting of the main present-opening (this usually takes a fair amount of time, owing to the quantity of gifts) and huge meals. The next few days are spent eating and relaxing. While some firms do not require their staff to return until the New Year, others are open for the last few days of December.

New Year's Eve
While Christmas is a family time, seeing the New Year in is more about friends. Romanians will have parties or go drinking in bars, restaurants, and nightclubs, with festivities continuing until 5:00 or 6:00 a.m. Midnight firework displays are popular in the towns; these often focus on the aesthetic element to the detriment of health and safety concerns,

and can be quite terrifying. In Bucharest, the gathering place of recent years has become Universitate Square.

Easter

Easter is the most important festival in the Orthodox Christian year. In the countryside various customs and rituals are observed in the run-up to Easter, but these are rarer in

the cities. Chief among these traditions is the painting, breaking, and eating of eggs. Boiled eggs are colored, and then smashed against each other, as the smashers say "Christ is risen" (*Hristos a înviat*) and "He is risen indeed" (*Adevărat a înviat*) in a traditional game. Other festive food includes lamb and a sweetbread called

cozonac. Christians attend church on Easter Saturday evening for the Night of Resurrection (*Noapte de Invierea*) service, with many staying there all night.

NAME DAYS

Many Romanians name their children after saints. On the particular day associated with a given saint, people who share the name will celebrate in much the same manner as they would their birthday. Children will bring sweets into school for their classmates, and if a few adults are celebrating together—some name days coincide—there may be a small work party. People also celebrate on the saint's day of their middle name.

Other Special Days

Early March is a good time to be a Romanian flower seller. March 1, officially the first day of spring, is known as *Mărțișorul*. Men traditionally give flowers or small gifts to all the women with whom they will have dealings that day. A small red and white lanyard is attached to the bunch, which the woman then pins on her clothing for luck. One week later the florists are busy again, for International Women's Day.

FROM BIRTH TO DEATH

Babies are typically named after a close relative, or after the name of the saint whose day is closest to the birthday. Most are given two prenames. A typical name would be Andreea Maria Ionescu or Ion (John) Andrei (Andrew) Popescu. The central core of Romanian names is fairly limited and well used, and there are very few cases of parents departing from the norm and imaginatively giving their offspring an unusual, foreign, or invented name. A newborn baby will be baptized, usually within its first few months.

The event will often be a big one, attended by the parents' family and friends and followed by a party. A couple is usually chosen to be the child's godparents.

Birthdays are big events for Romanians, offering a chance to forget the travails of daily life and celebrate among friends. If the party is held in a restaurant or bar, the custom is for the person whose birthday it is to pay for all the food and drink consumed. This might explain why not everyone chooses to celebrate their birthday! Guests are expected to bring presents, and flowers if the person celebrating is a woman.

A wedding is a huge deal in the life of most Romanians, who will probably have been encouraged to take this step by their parents for most of their lives. A civil ceremony, attended by close friends and family only, is followed a day or so later by a church service, after which a restaurant is booked for a big party. Instead of bringing presents, guests are expected to give cash—enough to cover their share of the cost (*tacâm*) plus some extra. Some foreigners—and Romanians—find this practice somewhat mercenary, and think it distorts the happy spirit of the occasion. Some couples invite rich acquaintances to the exclusion of closer, but less wealthy, friends. Indeed, while theoretically the couple should be happy for a poor friend to attend, even if he or she is unable to donate any money, in practice this is not always the case, and sometimes people will skip a wedding for financial reasons. Few people can afford to pay for a restaurant meal for several dozen friends, plus all the other wedding costs, so the system does allow poorer couples to marry without shouldering a large debt.

The party involves traditions such as the kidnapping of the bride, where male guests drive the bride away and return her in exchange for a "ransom," usually alcohol. Newlyweds also choose godparents—an older married couple who can give them advice—when they get married. In rural areas, the bride used to come with a dowry, which her parents had been setting aside for most of her life, although this is rare nowadays.

Funeral customs are another area of traditional Romanian life set to be altered by EU membership. While in the past it was traditional for the body to lie in an open casket in the home for three days after death, this will now have to happen in the church. After the church service, at which mourners approach the casket and say good-bye to the deceased—often rather dramatically—the body is buried. This is followed by some food, either at the cemetery or later at the house of the bereaved family.

chapter four

MAKING FRIENDS

To a Romanian, a true friend is an extension of the family, a person to welcome into your home and with whom to share confidences and possessions. Returning expatriates often complain that friendship outside Romania is colder and more distant—for example, that non-Romanians prefer you to call ahead rather than just drop by. In practice, though, many Romanians prefer their friends to phone ahead as well.

Because Romanian society is so couple-centric, as we will see further on, friendship can take a backseat for some once they find a partner. Socializing tends to occur mostly in sets of couples; while some single-sex groups of friends do spend evenings together, this is not as common as it is elsewhere. Some Romanians do form close, long-lasting friendships, but in times of need people are more likely to turn to their immediate family or their partner.

As well as school, college, and work, the local area also provides a significant source of acquaintances, and many friendship groups are composed largely of neighbors. Owing in large part to the suspicion fostered by the Communist system, adult Romanians tend not to make new friends that easily, and their social circles are made up of just a few people whom they have known a long time. However, this wariness does not extend to foreigners, who are pretty much guaranteed a warm welcome.

While making friends usually happens fairly quickly, it can take longer to adjust to Romanian manners, which can seem absent on occasions. People can be disarmingly direct, talk in loud, aggressive-sounding tones, interrupt, and seldom bother with a "please" or "thank you." It is better to get used to things before passing judgment: what initially seems like rudeness or boorishness often has an explanation, or is simply not considered bad manners in Romania. Once you have adjusted to this, your dealings with people will become much more pleasant.

HOW TO MEET PEOPLE

Romanians are friendly and open, particularly to foreigners, and you should have no trouble meeting people. Bars and nightclubs are standard places to meet others. Coworkers usually do some socializing together, so you are likely to get to know any colleagues reasonably well. Conversations can even spring up on public transportation, especially long train journeys, in shops, in parks, and on the street. In short, in most places a foreign accent will be enough to get you noticed and engaged in conversation. Romanian society is networkbased, with introductions and friends of friends facilitating a lot of business and personal connections. Once you make one friend, it is a small step to integrating into a whole bunch. The still limited extent of the expatriate community means that you will quickly get to know fellow foreigners, and everybody seems to know everybody else in one way or another.

FORMS OF ADDRESS

Traditional etiquette requires that a younger person greet an older person first, although few people other than the elderly still have this expectation. The convention is that a child should greet an adult, and a man a woman, by saying "Sărut-mâna," which translates as "I kiss your hand." Some old-school gents will accompany this with the described action and actually kiss the woman's hand, particularly in the smaller towns. Foreign men are not expected to do so. Many older people are very formal, and some can be overly particular about the greeting etiquette to the point of obstinacy.

Among younger people, the conventions are slightly different. There seem to be two kinds of greeting protocol. The first is slightly more formal or reserved. Upon arrival, the theory is that a man shakes hands with the men present and acknowledges the women with a nod and a "hello" of some form. In practice, the arriving man will often shake hands with the other men and totally ignore the women. Many Romanian women, used to their lower standing in society, seem to find nothing amiss in this procedure, but to foreign women (and men), it can appear enormously rude. Rudeness is not the intention, but such habits persist, although many people take it quite well if you confront them about it. Another gender difference is that young female friends sometimes hold hands in the street, which young men would never be seen doing.

The second type of greeting is much warmer and more intimate. Here, people will give each other a double (treble among certain groups) kiss on the cheek on arrival and departure. Unlike in Western culture, this is not restricted to women—men too will kiss both women and other men. If this is the established protocol among a group, it will be done to all attendees, even if they are newcomers, as it would be considered strange to exclude anyone. On a large group outing, this can make getting away a protracted process. Interestingly, given that Romania is generally a tactile country, hugs are very rare, and even an emotionally wrought, tearful parent greeting a returning child will do so with a double cheek kiss rather than a warm embrace.

Like greetings, terms of address vary. Friends and colleagues who know each other well generally use each other's first names, or sometimes surnames in an informal, jovial way. With people with whom they are less familiar, they might precede their first name with Mr. or Mrs. (*Domnul* or *Doamna*). These terms can also be used before someone's profession, as in *Domnul director* for "Mr. Director."

Like other Latin languages, Romanian has a formal and an informal way of addressing people, the former also being used in the plural. The single, informal word for "you" is *tu*, the plural *voi,* and the formal *dumneavoastră* . These pronouns are seldom actually spoken, however; rather, the form of the verb used indicates which pronoun is implied. For example, "you are" (informal, singular) is *tu eşti*, but it is normally expressed simply as *eşti*, and *voi* or *dumneavoastră sunteţi* expressed just as *sunteţi*. This can be awkward for foreigners unfamiliar with the system, faced with the dilemma of risking impertinence or implying an unfriendly distance. In general, the polite form *dumneavoastră* is used to someone of higher "status"—a category that includes older people and those in seniority at work or in a social situation—and the informal version *tu* for people of the same age or younger or in an inferior social position. This causes obvious incongruities. What if a shop assistant or waiter—a social "inferior"—is much older than you? On top of that, some people use the polite form when meeting any new person, except a child, for the first time, and expect the same in return. Serious arguments have been known to result from disputes over the wrong form of address.

Fortunately, foreigners have some leeway, and Romanians do not expect an outsider to be familiar with the convention. If in doubt, stick to the formal version—a Romanian who wants to deal with you on a friendlier and more relaxed basis will soon let you know.

TABLE MANNERS

The table manners of the average Romanian family may seem a little rough-hewn to an outsider. As we have seen, many urban Romanians have parents from the countryside, and often it is a case of rustic country ways looking a little uncouth in the city. Meals are often jovial, informal occasions, with few feeling the need to stand on ceremony. Family members rarely wait until the cook—in almost all cases the mother—is seated before they start eating, and will dig in as soon as they receive their portion. People may eat quite noisily and deposit bones and the like on the table itself. The upside of this is that Romanians tend to be relaxed about manners and etiquette in others, and you're unlikely to offend by using the wrong knife.

Expect to be offered seconds and even thirds. Refusals are usually interpreted as politeness rather than honest expressions of preference, and your host is likely to persist until you yield. Do not expect that asking for a little will make any difference to the amount you are given. Toasts are common, and there may be several throughout the course of the meal. When toasting, Romanians say "good luck" (*noroc*) or "to your health" (*sanatate*). They also use the same words after somebody sneezes, which is why some Romanians might say "cheers" to an English-speaker who has sneezed!

SMOKING

Anyone who intends spending time in Romania is going to have to get used to the fact that this is a smoking country. A huge proportion of people smoke here compared to the West, and attitudes toward the habit are very different. Few people will bother to ask if anyone minds before lighting up, no matter where they are. The one exception would be in the home of a nonsmoker, where they would most likely ask first. People will smoke while others are eating, in elevators and—perhaps the most upsetting to witness—around children, regardless of the obvious discomfort of others. Some offices still allow smoking.

Until a few years ago, the concept of a nonsmoking section was almost unheard of outside the top few hotel restaurants. The prospect of EU membership, demand from increasing numbers of foreign visitors, and a slow awakening to health matters began to change this, and today more and more restaurants and cafés in Bucharest have smoke-free areas, as required by EU law. Some may be smoke-free in name alone—there may be little or no partitioning from the smoking section—but it is still a great advance on the situation just a couple of years ago. Perhaps the tipping point came when Gregory's, a chain of cafés that were always full of puffers, inside which it was often difficult to breathe, gave over parts of its premises to nonsmokers. As a rule, the more upmarket a place is, and the more foreigners who patronize it, the higher the chance of it catering to nonsmokers.

Although a request to direct their smoke in another direction may surprise a Romanian, they are often quite cooperative and try to comply as much as possible. Even if you stick to restaurants and cafés with nonsmoking sections, however, smoke is unavoidable in the street, in taxis, and even in the home; the majority of Romanian housing complexes are so poorly constructed that smoke fumes commonly waft from one apartment to another via various pipes and gaps.

CONVERSATION

We have seen that if Romanians are interested in something, they will ask you about it. They also feel free to voice their own opinions, some of which may veer toward the politically incorrect. There is a saying that if you have three Romanians at a table, you will have four different opinions.

Romanians enjoy a good argument, although they often argue with passion and received wisdom rather than facts and intellectual rigor. Feel free to voice your own views, but don't expect to convert anyone to your way of thinking, regardless of any watertight arguments you might produce. Despite the general lack of conversational taboos, Romanians may be quite shocked if you admit to drug taking or homosexuality; their respect for foreigners will probably override that, however, and a lively debate should engender no bad feelings.

Other people are often a major topic of conversation. Whose son or daughter has gone to work abroad, who's in poor health, who's got a new job, house, or car, who's getting married, plus any anecdotes that illustrate the terrible state of society today, may all be shared. While better-educated and more well-traveled Romanians are likely to ply you with questions about your homeland, others will have very local horizons and may exhibit a very limited interest in the world outside their country, considering it of little relevance to their lives.

Subjects of conversation differ depending on the area. A Public Opinion Barometer commissioned by the Open Society Foundation in 2006 found that, in isolated villages, talk centers on health and family problems. In larger, more central villages, work, house, and social issues are the main topics. Residents of towns with populations between 100,000 and 200,000 discuss TV programs and sex lives, while those in larger cities talk about politics, social policies, and sports. Wherever you are, the scandalous, spiraling prices are always a hot topic.

Conversations are often conducted in a loud, informal manner. It is quite common for people to interrupt regularly and speak over each other, and this is not considered rude. If someone feels contempt for what another person has said they will feel no compunction in showing it, and many people use a wide array of interjections, facial expressions, and noises to convey their views. Views are stated directly and seldom cushioned with kind words, although, as usual, many Romanians are aware that outsiders may not be used to such bluntness and will soften their speech accordingly. Many people feel free to change the subject suddenly, rather than observe a few moments' silence to check that nobody has anything to add before doing so.

Joining in a conversation in the Romanian language can be tough, even if you have some knowledge of it. Because interaction with foreigners is a relatively new phenomenon, people here find it difficult to remember to speak slowly and use simple words. This is especially true if you are talking to more than one Romanian speaker, as the pace of the conversation will immediately pick up. Even when the language used is your own, it can be hard to break in and make your voice heard. The best idea is to abandon much of what you were taught as a child and to feel at liberty to butt in, cut people off, and talk over them when they try to do the same to you. This can be a huge social challenge, but otherwise you are likely to spend group outings contributing relatively little to the conversation.

Street-based conversations are often concluded as the participants are separating, so good-byes may be exchanged by shouting over a distance of several meters.

EDUCATION AND OPINIONS

Are Romanians well educated? Yes and no. The Communist emphasis on education has worked its way into received wisdom, but in Romania it applied to a certain kind of education only. Because the Ceaușescu regime wanted prestigious engineering and infrastructure projects to prove to the world the greatness of Communism, it needed workers capable of constructing them—it did not want its citizens developing inquiring minds or too much independent thought. The education system, therefore, taught certain skills, problem solving techniques, and behavior, without encouraging people to think very much for themselves. It could be argued that the regime wanted its people well trained rather than well educated.

The effects of this are evident today. While Romania produces impressive linguists and software programmers—disciplines that require one to learn rules and operate within them—the creative professions lag behind. Many young

Romanians display excellent general knowledge—
for example, plenty can recite famous poems by
heart—but are on shakier ground if asked to give
and justify their own opinions. Hearing foreigners
assert and defend their views, particularly
unorthodox ones, can unduly impress some
Romanians, especially younger ones.

On some everyday topics, however, Romanians
will almost always express an opinion rather than
admit ignorance on a subject. Do not assume that
because advice is presented with confidence, the
person offering it has any evidence or experience
to back up their viewpoint. The mind control
practiced by the Communist regime suppressed
any inclination to challenge the received wisdom,
and once people get an idea fixed in their minds,
little can dislodge it and they will voice it
repeatedly and with full certainty. If you get to
know Romanians very well, you may also find that
they have opinions on the most private and
intimate minutiae of other people's lives—even
regarding matters that you would not consider it
possible for people to have opinions on, such as on
which side a person should sleep in their bed.

LANGUAGE

Young Romanians mostly have excellent foreign
language skills. Immersed in American and
Western culture through music, TV, and film, they
have a constant supply of English to absorb. They
are also extremely well motivated, keenly aware

that to get a good, highly paid job they will either need to leave the country or work in a multinational company in Romania, with English skills being vital in either case. Many people are very keen to practice English with a native speaker—but there's a caveat. While speaking English to nonnative English speakers, Romanians are relatively relaxed about making errors; aware that a native speaker will notice all their mistakes, however, many of them feel embarrassed and are subsequently reluctant to talk. They seem unaware of the irony that their interlocutor's proficiency in Romanian is likely to be minimal, and that he or she will probably be impressed by the level of English they have achieved, regardless of any mistakes.

With older Romanians, usually from around thirty-five upward, the situation is different. People of this generation, schooled in the Communist era, were taught Russian and French, not English, and strict censorship laws denied them access to English-language radio, TV, and media. The upshot of this is that in this age group English is spoken at a much lower level. Many individuals and companies are trying to remedy this, with business English lessons proving very popular, but above a certain age, few people (apart from those who have had the opportunity to travel or study abroad) will have any degree of fluency and to converse with them you will have to make the effort to learn some Romanian.

Learning Romanian

Although Romanian is a Latin language—so any French, Spanish, or Italian will help—and phonetic, with simple spelling, its grammar makes it difficult to master. Another obstacle is the response you will get to your efforts. Romanians are not at all disparaging of foreigners' attempts to learn the lingo—on the contrary, they are supportive and delighted to hear your mangled sentences—but because their country was closed off to outsiders under Communism, their experience of non-Romanians speaking the language is practically nonexistent. Whereas any English speaker is used to hearing English spoken in numerous accents and with varying degrees of accuracy, this is something novel to Romanians, and their first instinct is to laugh. This is from delight rather than derision, but it can be rather off-putting, as can the tendency of fluent English speakers to reply to your efforts in English. Their lack of exposure to hearing their language spoken in different accents can also mean that Romanians are prevented from understanding you by the slightest discrepancy in pronunciation.

Despite this, the average Romanian will greatly appreciate your labors, and learning the language is usually a rewarding endeavor, giving you access to people and culture that you would otherwise be denied.

chapter five

THE ROMANIANS AT HOME

Lack of money, the high cost of travel, and family values have kept the home at the center of Romanian life. While the Communist-era buildings can be depressing, residents often put great effort into making their homes as pleasant as possible. It is not uncommon for extended families to live together, including grandparents who need care and adult children who cannot afford to move out.

A typical day starts with breakfast prepared by the mother, after which everyone heads off to school or work. Even the largest city, Bucharest, is relatively compact, so most people's journeys are far less than an hour, with the exception of people who travel between cities. In the past, many Romanians came home from work for lunch; now employees are more likely to have a sandwich at their desks or stay in the vicinity of their workplace. Few take their full officially allowed lunch hour, not wanting to appear lazy in front of their boss or colleagues, even if they are only playing solitaire on their computer. Evenings are spent mostly at home watching TV, with younger people going out to a bar or restaurant.

Older women tend to spend the most time in the house, while their husbands meet other local men in a nearby pub or just on the street. Food trends are following those in the West: while in the past Romanians ate a lot of fresh food, sourced from their gardens or the local market, supermarkets and junk food are making inroads.

HOUSE AND HOME

Romania's grim housing is one of the most visible legacies of the Communist regime. Monotonous, substandard, dehumanizing—the notorious apartment complexes in which the majority of urban dwellers still live continue to scar the towns and cities. Inside the apartments, the utilities were poorly installed and are subject to regular suspensions and mishaps, and the weak walls do little to maintain privacy or keep out neighbors' noise. The inhabitants do not let the poor design and living conditions breed disrespect for their homes, however, and the areas in and around the complexes feel perfectly safe and not remotely intimidating, as they would in

many Western cities. As well as keeping their own homes immaculate, many Romanians, particularly older women, decorate the communal hallways and stairwells with plants and stick up pictures of prettier places and rural scenes.

Apartments were generally allocated by the Communists according to one's job, with people who worked in the same place often living in the same complex, and higher-ups (through party credentials rather than professional excellence) getting the pick of the better properties. Most apartments are on the small side for the number of people living in them, and often the living room doubles as a bedroom for the parents. Part of the problem is high rents and the low availability of mortgages, which the average person cannot afford (or at least cannot prove that they can afford, as many firms declare only the minimum salary on people's wage slips to avoid tax). As a result, adult children routinely still live at home into their thirties and beyond. The noise level can be high, with clunking old elevators, loud music from other apartments, the beating of carpets outside (vacuum cleaners are not widespread), and neighbors' footsteps and DIY among the annoyances regularly endured by residents. Communism eroded privacy, and if you live in standard Romanian housing you should expect repeated visits from neighbors, who will often be well-intentioned and friendly.

If you are invited into a Romanian home, it is polite to remove your shoes—or at least to offer to—when you enter. The host will often have spare pairs of slippers for guests. Romanians seldom walk around barefoot, as they think doing so risks catching a cold, and will try to convince you to wear slippers too.

FOOD

Romanians—particularly the older ones—tend to be on the conservative side when it comes to food. Communist restrictions deprived the country of the opportunity to enjoy foreign foods and influences, and older people stick to a traditional diet of local, usually country, fare. Younger Romanians, with higher disposable income and more interest in the outside world, are slightly more adventurous, and enjoy going to restaurants that serve foreign cuisines, but the fact that the vast majority of such places are Italian, and the scarcity of more exotic options, indicate that the introduction to new gastronomy is a slow process. Chinese and Thai meals are enjoyed by a tiny minority of local people, and Asian restaurants tend to cater to foreign diners. The local conservative palate shuns anything spicy, and the international cuisine on offer may be far less piquant than the authentic version.

Romanian cuisine is predominantly meat-based, with influences from the Balkans and Turkey. Pork is the most popular meat, followed by chicken and beef, then by fish and lamb, although the lamb eaten in Romania is typically quite tough. Many vegetables are grown here, but they usually accompany the meaty main event rather than feature as meals in their own right, although there are a few honorable exceptions. Vegetarianism is unusual, veganism unheard of. Meals are typically hearty. They do not follow the "meat and two veg" model, and a "meal" may consist of just one or two constituent parts, like sausages, or sausages and fries or *mămăligă*, a maize dish. At other times, however, meals will be substantial affairs, with soup, salad, meat, and drinks, all accompanied by a good dose of carbohydrates—bread, fries, or maize. The Western concept of "healthy" is only just starting to make inroads in Romania. Expect food and drink to be served with copious amounts of salt, sugar, oil, and fatty sauces. These are often added before they get to the table, denying you the chance to choose whether you want them or not.

Specialties
Although foreigners can find the local food uninspiring, there are several enjoyable delicacies. *Sarmale* are rolls of rice, vegetables, and minced meat wrapped in cabbage leaves; they are eaten in various forms throughout the Balkans. *Salată de vinete* is roast eggplant or eggplant salad with onions, a delightful dish that is great on toast, and one of the national cuisine's concessions to vegetarians. Opinion is divided on *mici*, mixed meat sausages that hold a similar place in Romanian culture to the beef burger elsewhere—these are often served up at outdoor

celebrations, accompanied by beer. *Ciorbă de burtă*, or tripe soup, is something of an acquired taste, but several other soups are favorites among foreigners. Soups here tend not to be blended, as few people own mixers and blenders, but are more in the style of broths and consommés— liquid with solid ingredients floating in them.

Country Eating

On the back of globalization and modernization, supermarkets and hypermarkets are now gaining ground; the culture of markets and fresh food is still strong, however, particularly in the countryside. Many country households have enough land for some basic farming, growing tomatoes, cucumber, garlic, and onions, with some fruit trees and a few chickens. This means that if you get the chance to have a meal with a  rural family, you're likely to enjoy fresh, organic produce that was picked a few moments earlier. For anyone used to lackluster supermarket produce, this is a real delight.

ALCOHOL

Alcohol is an integral part of Romanian life and culture. Traditional folk songs are typically about getting together with friends and drinking until the sun comes up. Because the climate and soil are suited to viticulture, wine is cheap and plentiful and is an effective way to unwind and forget the hard toil of rural life. In the countryside, the day's drinking can start as early as breakfast time. Wine's hold on rural communities is nothing new: the Dacian king Burebista is said to have ordered all the vines in the area torn up in the first century BCE to raise his people from their drunken torpor.

While urban dwellers might not start so early, alcohol remains an integral part of their lives. A dry celebration would be unthinkable. People are excluded from taking part in the many cheery toasts that punctuate a meal if they are on soft drinks, to the extent that a Romanian will visibly recoil rather than clink glasses with a nondrinker. The reason is superstition, but this, plus the pressure that teetotalers will come under to "join in," can create quite an oppressive atmosphere for anyone who doesn't want to drink.

On top of this, drink is easily accessible in terms of price, venues, and store hours. Alcohol is on sale in a far wider range of outlets than in the West, including gas stations, the cinema, and even fast food joints like McDonald's and KFC. While imported brands are expensive, it is possible to buy local beer and spirits at low prices. There are no general restrictions on the

sale of alcohol (aside from its being prohibited for those underage), which can be bought twenty-four hours a day. Wine and beer are both popular, as is the traditional Romanian spirit *țuică* , a kind of pungent plum brandy.

Despite the ubiquity of alcohol, it is rare to see obviously drunken Romanians on the street. Scenes you might come across in Northern and Western Europe, with young people strewn around the city center, fighting, vomiting, and slumped on the ground, are unknown here. Perhaps the fear that people still have of authority makes them reluctant to indulge in unfettered self-expression and individuality. The legacy of the police state, where letting go and speaking freely could have serious consequences, could also be a factor.

Even rarer than a visibly drunk Romanian man is a visibly drunk Romanian woman. A double standard exists in that while it is generally accepted that getting drunk is something that men do, an inebriated woman is more of a scandal. It has even been reported that scenes from *Dallas*—tremendously popular in Romania in the 1980s—were edited to remove Sue Ellen's alcoholism, because women drinking was such a taboo.

HEALTH
Health is not a high priority for most Romanians. Drinking and smoking rates are high, and a fatty, salty diet contributes to one of the lowest life expectancies in Europe. Given the tough times

that people endured, it is easy to see why prolonging life became secondary to enjoying the moment with guilty pleasures. This was coupled with a general lack of health education, so that inaccurate knowledge was passed down the generations unchallenged.

The health care system has its problems. Struggling on pitifully low salaries, Romanian doctors have generally faced a stark choice: either abandon their local careers and head to the USA, Canada, or Western Europe, supplement their meager income with bribes, or live with their parents and give up all hope of a better standard of living. Despite this dreadful situation, there are some excellent, well trained, and committed medical staff working in Romania. Everybody has a horror story about a friend who was in an accident and had to pay a bribe before he or she could get treatment, but this is by no means always the case and there are plenty of Romanian medics who would not dream of asking for illicit payment. Facilities in hospitals may seem on the primitive side, but the treatment is perfectly adequate, sometimes even better than you would get in more advanced countries.

TELEVISION

At the center of Romanian home life is the television set. In some households it is on almost continuously from the time of the first member waking up to the last person going to bed. People rely on the TV for news as well as entertainment.

TV has established a stranglehold on Romanian life for both political and financial reasons. Under Communism programming consisted mainly of two hours a day of dreary propaganda supplemented by the odd socialist movie. When independent companies introduced new, international shows in the 1990s the public was thrilled, and watching TV became an enjoyable way to throw off the past. Low incomes put the cinema, opera, or having a meal in a restaurant beyond the means of many people. TV, on the other hand, was free entertainment.

Given this huge enthusiasm for TV, it is a pity that the vast majority of local programs are truly dire. One of the staples is the *telenovela*, a melodramatic type of soap opera imported from South America; Romania now has homegrown versions too. Other popular broadcasts are cheap copies of low-brow foreign imports such as *Surprize Surprize*, inane talent contests, variety shows, and anything reuniting estranged families. All are characterized by low production values, an overload of sentiment, and a sexist presentation of women. Fortunately, most Romanians have a cable TV package and get a full range of international channels such as the BBC, CNN, National Geographic, Animal Planet, and MTV.

THE FAMILY

The family is an important social unit, and Romanians typically have strong family ties. Many adult children still live at home, and while this is due in part to unaffordable housing, Romanian mothers often do little to encourage their offspring to leave the nest, providing a full service of cooked meals and all laundry done. Far from seeming anxious to have their own place, many Romanians in their twenties and thirties—particularly men—are quite happy to stay at home and be catered to. Interdependence usually takes precedence over independence in Romanian families. Grandparents, particularly widowed or ailing ones, also commonly live with one of their children's families.

These family bonds keep people in close proximity to one another. While many young Romanians do go abroad, either for a better salary or to further their career, plenty who are interested in the outside world reject the idea because it would mean being a long way from siblings and parents. While some young people move from their home town—usually to a bigger city to work or study—they still retain strong links with their parents, returning for regular weekend visits, often with dirty laundry in tow.

CHILDREN

Romania has a very child-friendly culture. Children are typically more indulged than in the West, which can be irritating if you're in a restaurant and

screaming children are running around unchecked
by their seemingly oblivious parents. Nobody
seems to have any concerns about the waiters with
bowls of hot soup weaving their way through a
sprawl of toddlers and toy trucks.
This child-friendliness is more
evident in attitude than in actual
facilities, however; most
restaurants lack high chairs and
children's menus, and what few
public playgrounds there are tend
to be rickety and run-down.

Because of the Ceaușescu
government's policies, which encouraged
mothers to return to work and leave their children
in day care, many women today go straight back
to work soon after giving birth and find the idea
of staying home to care for their children strange.
Gender socialization starts early. Baby girls are
decked out in pink and have their ears pierced so
strangers know they are female. As elsewhere,
educated and professional women tend to have
children later in life than uneducated ones.

EDUCATION
Romanian schooling comes in four main stages:
optional kindergarten (*grădinița* or *învățământul
preșcolar*); elementary school (*școala primară*) for
grades one to four and gymnasium (*gimnaziu*) for
grades five to eight; high school (*liceu*) for grades
nine to twelve or thirteen; and higher education

(*studii superioare*). Children start school at the age of six, and attendance is compulsory until the age of sixteen. High schools may be theoretical or technical. Private schools are now beginning to open, but represent a small percentage of the total and cater largely to expatriate children and the offspring of rich Romanians. Many families opt for private tutoring (*meditații*) to improve their children's chances of getting the grades required to get into a good university. Romanians often maintain friendships with classmates, particularly as they tend to remain living in the same area. There is an equivalent of Friends Reunited: www.colegi.ro.

Until 2006, male school graduates faced the prospect of mandatory military service. This could be delayed or avoided by further education or a medical certificate, which could sometimes be procured through connections. The majority of conscripts regarded their stint as a poorly paid waste of time, and national service seems to have done little to foster patriotism.

A COUPLE-CENTRIC SOCIETY

In the street, in the park, in the restaurant, in the supermarket—couples are everywhere in Romania. It is assumed that everyone must be looking for a mate, and single people, especially women, tend to be the objects of some pity and often clumsy attempts at matchmaking. Couples are expected to do most things as a unit, and too much independence or a separate social life can be read by others as a sign of something wrong in the relationship. It is expected that when someone is in a couple the time spent socializing with their friends will be cut, and this is not considered a reason to take offense.

MARRIAGE

Although, as throughout Europe, cohabiting is an increasingly popular choice, marriage remains the gold standard in religious, traditional Romania. Parents still hope for their children to get married, while the younger generation finds living together an acceptable alternative. Women are, on average, just over twenty-five at the age of their first marriage, men twenty-eight and a half. These figures have risen steadily. Divorce remains low by European levels, probably due to the country's strong religious morality and women's still limited economic opportunities. After divorce, lack of money forces some couples to stay living in the same house for years.

LOVE AND SEXUALITY

Sexuality runs through Romanian society. Perhaps due to Latin sensuality, perhaps as a reaction to the fall of Communism, perhaps because society it is still trying to work out its values, sex is all around you in Romania.

Passionate kissing and caressing are common in public, particularly in parks, which play host to lovers still living with their parents. Advertisers have yet to move beyond simply associating their products with a cleavage-baring woman. Many women dress in a surprisingly provocative way to Western visitors—even news anchors and businesswomen appear in low-cut tops, skirts that look more like belts, and heavy, obvious makeup.

But while the style of dress favored by some women would suggest that Romanians are a liberated, sexually confident people, this is not typically the case. Romania is a conservative country where religion still informs attitudes, and there is a fixed and narrow idea of what constitutes appropriate sexual behavior. Under Communism any discussion of sex was taboo—aghast parents rushed to protect their children from the mildest sexual content on TV, which was in any event vigorously censored—and as a result the younger generation grew up viewing sex as something shrouded in shame. This is now changing, with the young MTV generation being much more open and relaxed about sexual matters, which they discuss openly.

Despite increasing Westernization, prejudices still remain. Many Romanians, including young and educated people, are stridently homophobic. Bucharest does have a few venues for gay people, but the scene is nascent and an openly gay couple would be at risk of some hostility, or at least glares. Gay pride parades, which have taken place annually since 2005, routinely attract dramatic denunciations, missiles, and physical attacks from right-wing and religious groups. This highlights something that Westerners may perceive as an inconsistency in Romanian sexual mores. While a loving and equal gay partnership would be unacceptable to most people, Romanians take a more permissive attitude toward sexual relations that to an outsider might seem exploitative. One of the most popular TV programs is a reality show featuring a rich businessman of nearly fifty and his teenage wife, who is from a poor background. While some Romanians find the relationship distasteful, many others can see no problem and continue to enjoy the program.

Attitudes to prostitution are relatively lax. As in other countries with poverty and gender inequality, prostitution is visible despite being illegal, and many people regard it as a legitimate outlet for men, with little thought for the welfare of the women. It is not uncommon to find flyers for prostitutes on the table in upmarket-looking restaurants. Foreign men are at particular risk of being robbed by prostitutes and pimps.

Pedophilia is not discussed much, but the poverty and disastrous child policies of the Communist regime have left a legacy of vulnerable young people, and this coupled with an inefficient legal system has led to foreign criminals targeting Romania's street children and other youngsters. Fortunately, with European integration, child welfare is becoming a priority.

chapter six

TIME OUT

Romanians embrace their leisure time with gusto. With a harsh past and an uncertain future, they throw themselves into the present and live it up. Higher salaries and proliferating restaurants, bars, and new American-style entertainment options are opening up a plethora of new ways to pass the time away from the TV set. Alcohol often helps things along. Romanians are legally entitled to twenty-one days' leave from work, in addition to seven days of statutory holiday, but ambitious professionals often don't take the full entitlement.

ROMANIANS RELAXING

In contrast to Communist times, where provided one clocked in at work one could often be home again within a few hours without anyone complaining, today's Romanians work long and hard hours. As a result they like to make the most of their leisure time: weekends, from Friday evening to Sunday night, and public holidays are much looked forward to. A great deal of leisure activity involves going out in sets of couples—it is rare to see groups of female friends on a girls' night out, although young men do socialize together a bit more. The disparity is even more pronounced among older Romanians: while men gather to drink and smoke in small, basic pubs known as *birt-uri*, more mature women seldom meet for coffee or lunch (apart from breaks with work colleagues). Many men are keen gamblers, going to casinos and betting on far-flung foreign football teams they know nothing of, and slot machine arcades are a growth business area.

Romanians tend to socialize in conventional ways. Popular venues are bars, restaurants (often for special occasions), parks, and malls. Bowling and pool are also popular among the young. Most leisure activities are accessible to foreigners, as members of staff often speak some English. There are museums and galleries, particularly in Bucharest and the larger cities. More highbrow diversions, such as ballet, classical music, and opera, are all available for bargain ticket prices. Aside from that, money is the key differentiator: the proportion of foreigners is usually higher at the more expensive venues. Popular weekend activities for locals include trips to the mountains—and beach in the summer—and family picnics in nearby green areas.

RESTAURANTS

After the scarcity and poor quality of food under Communism, restaurants are now a popular novelty. The dominant fare is probably the national cuisine. Foreign foods are relatively new to the country, and as yet there is no tradition of experimenting with exotic new tastes. A few years ago expatriates bemoaned the lack of decent Asian food in the country, and if you wanted anything non-European you'd have been hard pressed to find it. This is changing with younger Romanians' increased access to foreign travel, and in the capital restaurants serving a wealth of different cuisines (*specifice*) are springing up all the time—although the trend is likely to take a long time to permeate the rest of the country. After local food, the second favorite is Italian. Leisure guides include listings of restaurants. While many come and go, there are several stalwarts in the major towns whose reputations are well deserved.

Local restaurant etiquette may come as something of a shock to foreigners. Chief among the gripes is the noise: tables tend to be packed in to maximize revenues, and there are often a couple of people whose unashamedly booming voices raise the general sound level. Employees may play loud music of their own choice that is inappropriate to the restaurant—thumping house music to accompany Sunday lunch in a beautifully decorated eatery, for example. This is exacerbated by cell phones. Few Romanians consider phones ringing loudly and being answered during a meal to be rude, and many are happy to conduct a thunderous conversation at the table while their companions continue to eat.

Children are routinely brought into restaurants, and with the local tendency to indulge rather than discipline unruly offspring, the result can be kids running around unchecked by parents who seem to feel that the restaurant is an extension of their living room. Other Romanians seem to find the spectacle sweet, and there is little to be done about it—even eating at a late hour does not guarantee that young children won't be present.

Another bane is smoke. As we have seen, nonsmoking sections are often very small and fill up quickly, and sometimes the separation from the smoking section is purely notional, meaning you are still going to get smoke with your food. Nonetheless, the current situation is a vast improvement.

The fourth typical visitor pet peeve with restaurants is the attitude of the staff. Many people worked for the state under Communism, and they retained their jobs through connections, not productivity. Nobody cared if their employer made money or not, and there was no incentive to work hard or well. This mentality has unfortunately been passed on, and it is common, even in the more upmarket restaurants, to struggle vainly to catch the attention of chatting waitstaff, or to be served by surly or inept individuals.

These drawbacks, though, must be set in context. While prices are rising, eating out in Romania is still a bargain. Expect an informal, fun environment rather than a sophisticated evening out, and have patience with the minor irritations, and you can enjoy some great food in a lively atmosphere. Among the top restaurants the service, style, and cuisine are as good as any in the West. Romanians usually like to divide the bill according to what they have consumed rather than split it equally—on their low salaries, they can rarely afford to be liberal with their money.

Some foreigners are embarrassed by the discourteous way in which certain Romanians address waitstaff. In a transition society where people may be insecure about their status, some individuals feel they can assert their position by speaking down to those they consider to be beneath them, such as workers in the service industry. While the employees are used to this behavior and are unlikely to be much put out, it can be awkward for foreigners not used to these scenes, who can do little other than be courteous and polite themselves.

In Romania, the term "restaurant" also extends to fast food outlets, which are incredibly popular. This is partly due to enthusiasm for all things American, but it is also a welcome change after putting up with such a homogeneous diet for so long. Romanians seize upon anything new from the West with fervor. Another advantage that fast food businesses have is that their standards of service, consistency, and hygiene compare favorably with other cheap eateries. With the health message slowly getting through and the novelty wearing off, however, the initial eagerness is now waning a little—but among some people a trip to McDonald's, KFC, or Pizza Hut is still a big event, and worth getting dressed up for.

TIPPING

Waiters tend to expect lower tips than is common elsewhere in Europe. Rounding up the bill or leaving slightly below 10 percent is the norm. Some Romanians tell the waiter how much to take by way of a tip when the payment for the meal is collected. Foreign visitors can find this awkward, and it is perfectly fine to leave the tip on the table when you go.

In a taxi, rounding up the fare is appreciated; a few drivers get nasty if this is not done. If you pay with a higher-value note, some drivers will hand you your change grudgingly, if at all, although the situation is getting better. Other professionals who appreciate a tip include hairdressers and beauticians, but some Romanians leave their small change to all manner of poorly paid employees, from hospital staff and postal workers to shop assistants.

When tipping in general, rounding up the bill is usually sufficient, unless it comes to a very small sum or the service was exceptional. In better restaurants and more international venues you may wish to leave around 10 percent.

CLUBS AND BARS

Romanians started celebrating after the revolution in 1989, and do not seem to have stopped since. Nightclubs are often packed (sometimes to the point of enforced immobility) and lively, with a sizable percentage of the crowd still going strong at closing time, which can be as late as 5:00 a.m. Most people dance for most of the night, and although a lot of alcohol is consumed, the atmosphere is generally a happy one, unsullied by drunkenness or violence. Clubs can be incredibly smoky, and sometimes you wouldn't want to give too much thought to the health and safety aspects, but in general they are spirited places and can be a lot of fun. Many venues, particularly basement clubs, are cheap and unpretentious, but Bucharest has a few self-consciously trendy superclubs that fly in top international DJs. These are the places where the city's poseurs (*fițoși*) go to see and be seen. Foreign visitors tend to go to such venues for the comedy value, rather than earnestly—if you do want to get in, you have to look the part.

Bars vary from basic, men-only (in practice, if not officially) canteens selling cheap draft beer, wine, and spirits to plush international-style cocktail lounges where the prices differ little from Western

capitals. What most have in common is smokiness. Romania has fairly liberal licensing laws: if you want to keep drinking all night long you can usually find a place to do it, at least if you're in a larger city. There is no tradition of buying rounds; people order what they want—the vast majority of places have table service—and the bill comes at the end of the night when, unless someone is playing host and therefore paying, it is divided according to individual consumption.

BATHROOM ETIQUETTE

Two quirks of bathroom etiquette may come as a surprise to the first-time visitor. If it is unclear whether a cubicle is occupied (locks are often old-fashioned bolts and seldom have a red indicator or "occupied" sign), a person waiting will knock on the door. This is considered a practical necessity, not an intrusion. Clearly any reply you give will suffice to convey your presence, but the usual response is "*ocupat*," meaning "occupied."

The other thing to be aware of is that some Romanian women stand, rather than sit, on the toilet seat in public conveniences, and assume a crouching position similar to that required for a squat toilet (very rare in Romania, and almost nonexistent in major cities). This perilous maneuver is prompted by their fear that the seat is dirty. The result is that in a nightclub, it can be covered in grimy footprints, rendering it unusable. Fortunately, the practice is quite rare and you won't find it in upmarket places.

AT THE MALL

Representing consumerism, wealth, and the West—everything people were denied access to by the Communists—malls are beloved by young Romanians. If you refer to a shopping center that existed prior to 1989 as a mall, you will be corrected—even if nobody can point out the difference. Romanians are adamant that the mall "concept" is a modern one. Some people get dressed up to go to the mall—it is taken very seriously. Buying things is a small part of the occasion; it's more about the experience and, for some, the social cachet. Mall food courts are almost constantly packed. Most malls have entertainment in the form of amusement arcades, bowling alleys, and cinemas, although the movie audiences are generally there for something to do at the mall rather than specifically to see the film; concentration levels can therefore be low and chatting frequent, which can be irritating if you're interested in the feature.

THE CINEMA

Talking is a big problem in most cinemas in Romania. While the vast majority of people sit quietly, a significant portion cannot, enough to ensure that there will be talkers in almost all but the most highbrow or tragic films. Cell phones ring—and are answered. A shush sometimes shames a talkative viewer into silence for a short time, but noise levels soon rise again. For this reason it is best to avoid mall multiplexes and stick to art films or other serious features unlikely to appeal to the kind of person who talks all the way through a movie.

On the positive side, foreign features in Romania are subtitled, not dubbed. Most movies reach Romania fairly soon after their release in Western cinemas. Prices are low in comparison to other European countries, although tickets at mall multiplexes may only be slightly lower than the cheapest cinemas elsewhere. Non-mall movie theaters vary between the plush and modern and the delightfully archaic. Some of the latter offer rock-bottom rates, particularly for early screenings or Monday and Tuesday shows. The state also funds a handful of cinemas that show an impressive range of pictures, from eighty-year-old German silent films to Hollywood classics and quirky modern features. Film festivals on everything from Algerian movies to football-themed pictures take place regularly. Such events attract an eager, educated audience who sit silently throughout, which makes a pleasant change from the mainstream venues.

THEATER, OPERA, CONCERTS, AND JAZZ
If you're not expecting the variety and tradition of London or Paris, Bucharest enjoys a flourishing arts scene. While the majority of plays may be of limited interest to non-Romanian speakers, there is the odd performance in English. Consult listing

guides and magazines to see what's on—they are full of drama, concerts, opera, ballet, and art exhibitions. The most expensive ticket would be unlikely to set you back as much as US $10. Stadium concerts by visiting stars, which are now fairly common in the capital, cost slightly more, but are still far cheaper than in the West. Jazz fans are also well catered to, with regular gigs showcasing traditional and more experimental music. Expect to breathe in a lot of smoke.

The main arts venues are equally impressive. The National Theater is an imposing, modern, 10,000-square-meter building built by a group of local architects. Located in the middle of Bucharest, it hosts exhibitions and trade fairs as well as the country's top drama. Up on the roof is a very popular summertime bar. The Opera (it is never called an Opera House) is a plush, opulent auditorium, completed by socialist-realist designer Octav Doicescu in 1953, which recalls the capital's bygone glory days. Classical concerts are also staged at the neoclassical Athenaeum, possibly the country's most beautiful building.

PARKS

On a warm weekend or public holiday, the main parks and gardens are packed with playing children, cavorting couples, and groups of elderly friends watching the world go by. There are boating lakes, cafés and bars, children's playgrounds—in short, something for everyone. Less crowded parks host informal football matches, and their pathways a hybrid game of football-tennis. They are extremely well tended, and in spring come alive with planted floral displays. The best thing about parks in Romania is that they are often populated until late at night, with couples out for a midnight stroll and drinkers finishing up at the cafés, and they also have security guards, so they do not become the preserve of gangs of youths and drug dealers as can happen elsewhere.

There are only two downsides. In the smaller parks nobody is allowed on the grass, and venturing on to it may get you scolded—possibly even fined—if a guard sees you. The other irritation is amorous young men who see parks as good places to pick up women, so a lone young female trying to read or just enjoy the sunshine will often be subject to annoying approaches from hopeful admirers. Such people are usually harmless, but can be persistent and may refuse repeated requests to be left alone. In such a situation it is better not to engage in conversation but simply to move elsewhere.

SPORTS AND PASTIMES

For Romanians, sports are usually about watching rather than participating. Football (soccer) is passionately supported, and derby games, involving any of the three major club sides—Rapid, Steaua, and Dinamo, all based in Bucharest—or the national team, engender strong emotions.

Such vociferous support has largely been undeserved—and unrewarded. Despite having some talented players, Romanian football has been held back by corruption, the poor habits of some players, and lack of professionalism among agents and the people in charge of the game, many of whom are dubious "businessmen" with little football knowledge who routinely sack coaches on a whim. The result of this is years of underachievement. Football fans like to hark back to when the national side beat England in Euro 2000 and Steaua's European Cup victory in 1986. There's little for them to boast about today. The game is so riddled with corruption that foreign referees are routinely used for big matches as a local official would almost certainly be bribed by a rich club chairman.

Watching football in Romania can be enjoyable—with some caveats. There's always a lively atmosphere, and some of the comments shouted at the players can be amusing, if profane. Tickets are cheap—as well they ought to be, given the quality of the football and facilities. Stadiums are generally old and decrepit, and the game is still plagued by hooliganism. On TV, coverage is routinely interrupted by quick commercials, and ads are beamed on to the screen from time to time—typical of the lack of respect that those in charge have for the loyal supporters.

With Western health and fitness concerns slowly permeating the country, there are a growing number of gyms (which Romanians refer to as "fitness") offering equipment, aerobics (popular with women trying to lose weight), and sometimes massages and saunas. Gym goers are often businesspeople. You can also find facilities for tennis and five-a-side football, although these are relatively expensive to hire by local standards. At present the country has only one golf course to speak of, in the Prahova Valley, which has nine holes, but the increasing number of foreign businessmen in Bucharest has boosted demand and more are currently under development. On the more cerebral side, checkers and chess are hugely popular, probably due to the Communist encouragement of chess (Lenin called it the "gymnasium of the mind"). You often find impromptu games on the street, and organized meets— exclusively involving old men—in places like Cismigiu Park in Bucharest.

VACATIONS

Because foreign travel has only recently become a realistic prospect for most people, vacations have generally been limited to domestic destinations—either the seaside or the mountains. (There is also the Danube Delta, but high prices and undeveloped tourist facilities have held that area back.) When one can and cannot go also seems to be fairly regimented: Romanians talk of the first or last suitable weekend of the season for going to the seaside (a weather-based assessment, with the assumption that nobody would think of going to a beach when it is cold).

Both areas have much in their favor. The Black Sea beaches are sandy, and the sea temperature is usually warm enough for a dip in season, but the tourist resorts lack decent infrastructure and have a tacky feel, while the beaches quickly get covered in litter. The resorts are also expensive; many Romanians find it cheaper to go to Bulgaria or Greece. Foreigners are particularly liable to be

ripped off. The mountain areas offer fine scenery, hiking, and skiing opportunities, but also suffer from high prices and poor service. Despite the drawbacks, the Romanian fun-loving spirit usually triumphs, with people flocking to the resorts and having a fine time there.

DRESS CODES
In the wake of Communism fashion trends spread through the country, particularly among the urban populace, and there is a certain homogeneity in how people dress. Many young Romanians,

particularly the more educated and traveled ones, have adopted the standard Western dress code of jeans and sneakers.

As we've seen, some Romanian women dress in a sexually provocative way that astonishes foreign visitors. This is not limited to nights out; it's common to see women teetering around the supermarket in heels and a miniskirt on a Monday morning, reflecting the huge emphasis placed on a woman's physical appearance and the thinking that her priority should be to look "sexy." Even bitter winter weather fails to persuade some women to put on more than the flimsiest of garments. It's also partly a reaction to the Communist period, when decent cosmetics and clothing were not readily available. Clothes came in standard, drab colors and styles, and any individuality would require the work of a tailor—although too much would have been frowned on.

Menswear is more closely aligned to Western norms, with jeans, sneakers, and T-shirts popular for casual occasions and business suits for work. Subgroups such as the Roma have a more distinctive style—rather than looking West for tips, they look East, and much of their clothing has a Turkish flavor. Many of the women still wear long, colorful gypsy skirts.

If you're going out for a special occasion, it's usual to make an effort with your appearance—although foreigners' idiosyncrasies are tolerated, and if you turn up looking casual bordering on scruffy it is unlikely that anyone will mind much.

chapter seven

TRAVELING

Thanks mainly to EU funds, Romania's network of largely potholed roads is slowly being repaired. Despite the usual controversy over the awarding of contracts, there are now some highways of a decent standard, and these are bringing journey times around Romania down.

Public transportation often brings you into close contact with local people. In some cases, such as sociable long-distance train journeys, where family photos, opinions, and snacks are shared around the car, this can be a pleasant distraction. In other instances, like being squashed, sardine style, into a jam-packed Bucharest bus and missing your stop because there's no prospect of reaching the door, it is less welcome. The good thing is that travel in Romania (with the exception of planes) remains one of the country's true bargains.

ARRIVAL

The majority of foreign visitors will fly into Bucharest's Otopeni Airport. In 2004 its name was changed to Henri Coandă International

Airport, after the Romanian flight pioneer, but this fact seems to have passed most people by, and it is still universally referred to as Otopeni.

In the recent past, the typical airport experience involved surly staff, long lines, chaos, and a phalanx of unofficial taxi drivers waiting for a gullible foreigner to transport to the city center for about ten times the proper fare. Since 2002 the authorities have tried to conform to international standards. One company was selected to provide an official airport taxi service;  admittedly it's one of the capital's most expensive firms, won a dubious tender, and had links with the government at the time. On the plus side, the cars are decent and have working seat belts, and although fares are still far too high they are same for all passengers. The alternative, cheaper means of getting between town and the airport is the 783 bus, which leaves from in front of the domestic terminal. Tickets must be bought from the kiosk at the bus stop and validated in a machine on board. A metro link to the airport is planned.

Since Bucharest has started to feature on the cheap flight network, some visitors are now arriving at the city's smaller airport, Baneasa. The advantage of this is that, unlike most airports used by low-cost airlines, it is much nearer to the city center than the main hub. At times, Baneasa can be relatively quick and painless to transit; however, if you are unlucky enough to pass through when a few planes are coming or going simultaneously, proceedings can be protracted. Many of the more disreputable taxi drivers ousted from Otopeni seem to have made their way here, and it is far better to book a cab or take the bus than chance a ride with the drivers outside.

WALKING

Even the largest city, Bucharest, has a small center, relatively easy to traverse on foot. Many of Romania's prettiest places are unpublicized, and walking is a great way to discover delightful streets, gardens, and buildings. One of the main barriers to a pleasant stroll is the state of the sidewalks. While the authorities are slowly getting around to repairing the road network, the sidewalks remain neglected, full of holes and bumps. Even decent sidewalks in the city are often blocked by cars parked directly across them, forcing pedestrians into the road—where motorists then honk their horns at them.

BUSES AND STREETCARS

Buses and streetcars are the main form of public transportation in the larger cities. In Bucharest the system is comprehensive and often quick, although of course it is subject to the vicissitudes of the traffic. You rarely have to wait long during the day; night services are less frequent. Tickets are sold from kiosks by most bus and streetcar stops until around 9:00 p.m. on weekdays and early afternoon on Saturdays, and must be validated on board. Monthly passes are available.

The flip side of their cheapness, frequency, and relative efficiency is that buses and streetcars often become uncomfortably packed, to the extent that the doors are barely able to close and faces and bodies are pressed up against the glass. Even the newer Mercedes buses have no air-conditioning, so in summer traveling at rush hour can be an ordeal. The crowded conditions also make public transportation fertile territory for pickpockets.

THE METRO

The cheapest form of public transportation is Bucharest's underground train system, known as the metro. It is usually more civilized than the aboveground options, and rarely reaches the extremes of crowdedness that are typical on streetcars and buses. Journey times are more predictable, and it is often the best way to cover long distances. The only logistical downside is that the network is not as comprehensive. The city is in the process of renewing its fleet of trains, which means that the tracks are currently shared by old graffiti-covered cars that look like something out of 1980s New York, and sleek and pristine new trains. The latter are protected against would-be graffiti artists by security guards, who rather than providing a reassuring presence are often more intimidating than the hoodlums they are meant to be deterring.

Foreign visitors will find a few other frustrations when traveling by metro. At busy stations, in their haste to get on, the waiting passengers will crowd around the door when the train arrives, thereby allowing only one person to disembark at a time, rather than the three who would be able to do so if the doorway were left clear. This slows things down somewhat. Escalator use can be another annoyance for anyone in a hurry—although in theory the "stand on the right" rule applies in Bucharest, in practice few people bother to observe it. Invariably, one person will stand on the left, blocking the progress of the line of people behind.

TRAINS

Long-distance trains come in four categories: *personal*, *acelerat*, *rapid*, and intercity. *Personal* services, the slowest and cheapest, make frequent stops in the remotest of outposts. They should only be considered if funds are tight or if you can view them as an interesting cultural experience. The latter is possible; they do tend to carry the chattiest passengers—probably because the journeys are so long they need to do something to pass the time. At the other end of the scale, the intercity trains, while still relatively good value, are either plush, modern, or both, with the first-class compartments rivaling the best for comfort and service. If you're traveling abroad or over a long distance in Romania, sleeper cars can be a good option, although there's a distinct difference in service and attitude on trains heading west of Romania and trains heading east, north, or south. Whatever train you're on, the one thing likely to be missing is a decent buffet car, so it is worth taking your own provisions.

TAXIS

Although taxi fares have soared in recent years, they are still much lower than in Western countries. Taxis can be booked by phone or hailed in the street; the former is preferable as you do not run the risk of being massively overcharged by a driver with a rigged meter. Most drivers will activate their meter automatically, but if they don't it's better to request it than to get into an argument at your destination. Romanian cab drivers in general, and Bucharest ones in particular, have something of a reputation for lying, cheating, taking circuitous routes, smoking, and driving recklessly. Some deserve this, but you will also find plenty of sane, friendly, and honest examples. Some of the very worst

congregate around the Gara de Nord, both airports (but particularly now Baneasa), and the Hilton Hotel. Unsolicited offers of a taxi in these areas should be firmly declined. As we've seen, it is usual to give a small tip at the journey's end.

DRIVING

Romania's road system is a chaotic, dangerous, illogical nightmare. The incessant hooting, lack of respect for pedestrians, and counterproductive blocking of the way are unfathomable and frustrating. Bucharest sees the worst of it. Motorists are typically aggressive and impatient, hooting a second or two after the lights change if the car in front does not immediately move. Many will even sound the horn if it is obvious that the road is blocked and nobody can go anywhere. As soon as one horn sounds, several other drivers will join in, as if not to do so would be proof of weakness. Drivers routinely block intersections, rather than wait for the way to clear, in the hope of making the light, even though this clearly brings no benefit and holds up other lanes of traffic.

Pedestrians have it worst. The amber light sometimes allows drivers to proceed if a pedestrian crossing is clear. In practice this means that while you cross, cars will edge as close to you as they can get, often honking their horns at you despite the fact that you have the right of way. When they do deign to stop, it is often on the crossing, rather than before it, forcing people to walk around them. Many drivers will not wait for a pedestrian to cross, even if a red light or traffic is preventing them from going anywhere.

FLYING

The cost of flights is hugely prohibitive for most Romanians. Only now is this changing, slowly, as Bucharest and Timișoara are beginning to feature on the low-cost flight network. As a result many Romanians you may share planes with are first-time flyers, which can lead to faux pas such as standing immediately behind the person being seen by the passport official rather than behind the painted line, leaping up to retrieve bags from the overhead lockers while the plane is still taxiing, trying to use cell phones on board, and general pushing and rushing. This stems mostly from panic about being in a new, intimidating situation, and is not deliberate rudeness. Once settled in their seats and enjoying the in-flight alcohol and coffee, most Romanians are as open and chatty as they are on other forms of public transportation. Groups of Romanians generally greet the successful landing of the plane they are on with a round of applause.

HEALTH, CRIME, AND SECURITY
Health

No inoculations are currently required to travel to Romania, but it is worth double-checking with your doctor a few weeks before you go. The food is unlikely to present a problem, and while the water is safe to drink it does not taste particularly good and most people buy bottled.

The level of medical treatment is fine. Reciprocal agreements with several countries, including the USA, Canada, and Australia, entitle their nationals to free emergency medical treatment. Holders of a European Health Insurance Card can access state-provided healthcare at a reduced cost or sometimes free. Even if you have to pay, simple procedures at a public hospital, where you should present yourself, are not usually expensive. For others, private health insurance is recommended. There are private clinics that meet international standards, although these tend to be in the big cities, and in rural areas facilities are lacking. Most medics speak English.

Stray dogs remain a problem—a by-product of the mass rehousing of the Communist era. Some people regard them as pets and feed them, and the animals are generally a nuisance rather than a danger, but they do sometimes bite. Some people carry biscuits to throw as a diversion. It is best to avoid deserted streets and other areas where packs congregate. If you feel threatened by a dog, walk away from it slowly, avoiding eye contact. Rabies exists in Romania, but is not widespread.

Security
In general, traveling in Romania is safer than in most European countries. Bucharest is far less violent than comparable cities, and muggings are

rare. The most trouble you're likely to encounter is of the nonviolent, sneaky kind: pickpocketing and low-level scams aimed at foreigners, most of them perpetrated by the most hapless of would-be con men. Women are more likely to be subjected to low-level hassles. Groups of youths will often play silly pranks when a lone woman walks past, such as shouting loudly to make her jump or jumping in her way to force her to walk around. Younger women may be subjected to inane approaches from men, in the vain hope that this will result in a date. These encounters are seldom dangerous, but can be very annoying. If you're walking alone it's better to cross the street and avoid any dubious-looking groups of males. A persistent admirer may go away if ignored—otherwise, it is better to move on.

If you should have the misfortune to be robbed or scammed, report it to the police. It is unlikely the perpetrator will be apprehended—although the police may be more inclined to act if the victim is foreign or persistent—but you may need the documentation to make an insurance claim.

The other main threat to safety in Romania is traffic. Erratic and aggressive drivers, old Dacias with substandard brakes, and the lack of road sense of some motorists combine to create dangerous chaos on the roads. While traffic in the city centers is likely to be too slow-moving for accidents to be serious, many intercity highways lack median strips and the two opposing high-speed lanes of traffic see frequent fatal crashes.

chapter eight

BUSINESS BRIEFING

THE CHANGING ECONOMY

The socialist economies of Eastern Europe were rife with inefficiencies, injustices, and abuses. Romania's economy suffered the further burden of Ceauşescu's drive to pay off the national debt by exporting the bulk of production, leaving the country criminally short of basic necessities. Romanians had a saying, comparing the state of their country during and after Communism: "Then, we had money but there was nothing in the shops to buy. Now the shops are full and we have no money to buy anything with."

Today, the outlook has been transformed. The economy is growing rapidly thanks to foreign investment and the vote of confidence of EU accession. Many state-owned, often loss-making, companies are being privatized, and while the process has attracted accusations of bribery and corruption, international investors seem largely undeterred. Foreign direct investment in Romania is among the highest in the region, although it may be tailing off as the majority of the large privatizations have gone through. Austria's Erste Bank and OMV, French carmaker

Renault, and India's Mittal Steel have been responsible for some of the biggest takeovers. The economic situation is becoming increasingly stable, and international ratings agencies have responded by raising Romania's score.

THE DACIA

The flagship product of the old Communist economy was the Dacia car. Despite its obvious deficiencies, Romanians took great pride in the odd-looking vehicle, which in its heyday had long waiting lists, and it remains one of the country's most loved brands—at least among the patriotic. The transformation of the Dacia is also a good illustration of the development of the economy at large. The original inferior plant, hampered by a lack of modern technology, was bought in 1999 by Renault, who invested heavily in it. Models of the vehicle quickly  improved, and the latest version, the Dacia Logan, released in 2004, is selling well and even being exported to the West. Some call it the first Dacia that actually looks like a Western car, and there is now a great deal of hope and optimism regarding the company's future prospects.

One boom area is real estate. Because the majority of Romanians live in grim Communist-era apartments, developers have seen their rising purchasing power as an opportunity. Malls, office buildings, and logistics facilities are also popping up all over the country. The general dearth of services, infrastructure, and businesses before the revolution has led to similar growth across the economy. The still low wages, young people's language skills, and the country's position by the Black Sea are further pulls for foreign companies.

Despite this buoyancy, there are concerns. Inflation is still high. While EU accession brings funds and opportunities, it also opens up the market to foreign entrants, most of whom will be far more advanced and competitive than local firms. At the same time new legislation imposed by the EU, particularly in the areas of health, safety, and the environment, requires a

lot of money to be spent on changing equipment and procedures, which many firms will not be able to afford. Most analysts predict mergers and bankruptcies and expect local companies to struggle in the liberalized market. While there will undoubtedly be casualties, the Romanian market remains an exciting and hotly tipped one. Rising living standards are making the country—more specifically, the capital—an acceptable place for foreign executives to work in. And while Western markets are closer to the saturation point, in Romania it is still possible to come up with a new idea and make a success of it.

BUSINESS CULTURE
While Romania was once considered something of a "Wild East," the business environment is becoming more equitable and stable. This is largely due to EU intervention, as well as pressure from foreign business lobby groups such as the Foreign Investors Council. Although the corporate world is aligning itself with Western practices, however, this is still a country in transition and unpredictable things happen.

Degrees of Formality
In some Romanian companies, particularly state-run or locally managed ones, formality prevails. Suits are worn, meetings scheduled far in advance, handshakes and business cards exchanged, and protocol is followed strictly. This level of decorum will continue until you get to know your associates better, after which they may relax things. In multinational firms and less formal businesses, such as media or IT, where the staff

tend to be young, things can be quite different. The uniform here is more likely to be jeans and sneakers, employees may put up posters, and there is a high degree of informality among the staff.

Do not try to use humor to set people at ease in negotiations, as it does not always travel. Avoid irony; people may not detect it, and may interpret light-hearted self-deprecation as a genuine admission of weakness.

Working Practices

Traditional business hours are from 9:00 a.m. to 5:00 p.m., but nowadays there is more flexibility; many people stay in the office until later in the evening, and may invite you for meetings up to around 8:00 p.m. Romanians work an average of eleven hours a day. While some employees do devote much of their lives to their work, the culture of work avoidance that grew up under Communism, when there was no incentive to be productive, is often evident.

Some companies close for several weeks in August, and high summer is not the best time to make appointments or get things done; the same applies to Christmas and Easter.

BRIBERY AND CORRUPTION

Romania's history of corruption predates the Communist regime—although, needless to say, that didn't improve matters. The country ranks far down the transparency league tables, and is considered one of the most corrupt in Europe. The arrival of international companies, with their Western standards, relative transparency, and codes of ethics, has helped to change things, but unfortunately many foreign firms seem to embrace the maxim "When in Romania, do as the Romanians do," and leave their business ethics at Otopeni Airport. Some international businesses— including famous global names— commonly dodge taxes, pay bribes, and commit misdemeanors that they

would not dare do in their home countries. Far from setting an example, these companies further disillusion their young, local workforce, who often describe their bosses as "more Romanian than the Romanians."

The victim of much of the corruption is the state—that is, the Romanian people. State officials are often poorly paid and retain a Communist mentality. A typical example of corruption might see a company pay a bribe to ensure it wins a government tender, with a million-euro cut going to the officials who facilitate the deal. Of course, another company could often have performed the work better, and for less money. The result of this is a few state paper pushers who earn, on paper, a modest salary and live in huge villas, plus a substandard and costly white elephant project foisted on the public and a large dent in the state coffers. Businesses pay bribes to middlemen and facilitators, without which there is precious little chance of the deal going through.

That said, the situation is improving. Many of the younger generation are thoroughly frustrated with the corruption, and bring a modern, more ethical attitude to their dealings. This is partly fueled by their ability to travel; whereas their parents' generation knew only the local reality, they have seen how business is conducted abroad. The country's EU aspirations have also been a spur to clamping down on graft, and the strict EU monitoring process makes it more difficult to get away with nefarious practices. This is not to say that Romania is now corruption-free (particularly not the state sector), but as younger, more open-minded, and optimistic people take over from the old guard, it is on the right track.

Part of the reason that corruption has flourished has been Romania's passive civil society. Older people are conditioned to corruption, and the oppressive and brutal governments of the past stamped out any public inclination to protest—but the emergence of NGOs has been a positive force, with many groups calling attention to corruption and pressing for action against it.

CONNECTIONS

While multinational companies in Romania operate much as they do elsewhere, in smaller firms connections and personal relationships take on great significance. In all walks of life, not just business, Romanians have difficulty in trusting strangers. Friends, lovers, business partners, lawyers, and accountants may all be chosen from within a close-knit social circle. The thinking seems to be, "Better the devil you know." Most businesspeople have at least one story about being ripped off or conned when they hired or dealt with an outsider, and they seem to conclude that they have a better chance of gauging the character of someone who is not a stranger. For this reason, connections in business are vital.

A Romanian business partner will have to learn to trust you before doing business with you, and it can take time to build up this relationship. An introduction from a mutual contact will certainly help. If you are negotiating on behalf of your company, your Romanian associates will consider the relationship to be with you rather than your firm. If you have to be replaced, the process of trust building has to start over. In this situation try to introduce your replacement to your associates.

This value placed on connections means that when hiring staff, Romanian bosses look far more favorably on applicants recommended by people they know rather than respondents to an advertisement in the media—although companies do make use of both systems. A foreigner first arriving in Romania and not knowing anyone may initially find it difficult to get work.

BUREAUCRACY

Romania is still burdened with a spirit-crushing bureaucracy. The simplest task, which should take a few minutes, can drag on for hours or days. Sometimes the inconvenience can be circumvented with a bribe, but in many cases the system just works frustratingly slowly. Under Communism, any initiative was stamped out, and with no incentive to improve things people acquired the habit of accepting the status quo.

The most bureaucratic institutions tend to belong to the state. Civic buildings have changed little since the Communist era. Operating hours, procedures, and attitudes leave a lot to be desired. The main victims of this are entrepreneurs. Large companies can afford to send employees to stand in line all day to get whatever document is required, but the small business owner will find that an awful lot of time gets eaten up in the performance of such tedious necessities.

THE BUREAUCRACY BUSINESS

The symbol of bureaucracy in Romania is the stamp, needed for a vast range of official documents in various aspects of business life. Romania's bureaucracy has its own flourishing industry—a chain of shops called Ştampile Express (Stamps Express) boasting outlets all over the place selling stamps and the other paraphernalia of bureaucracy.

Fortunately, the multinational companies in Romania are changing things. They typically start off with foreign CEOs, who train their workforce in Western business practices before handing over to local managers. While these companies have little influence over the state bureaucracy, at least their own procedures are less cumbersome and fairly similar to the international norm.

THE BLACK MARKET

Under Communism, Kent cigarettes served as a second currency and were exchanged for much-needed goods. The period had a profound effect on the public mentality, and much black market activity continues unabated.

One of the main areas involves infringement of copyright and intellectual property rights. Designer sports gear and alcoholic spirits were prohibitively expensive; this, coupled with weak law enforcement, led to a thriving black market for fake versions of such goods, some of which even made their way into apparently respectable shops. Today, computers and the Internet are a source of contraband intellectual property. Few see anything wrong with downloading or file sharing films and music. The majority of software continues to be pirated—pirate copies of DVDs, CDs, games, and software are easy to come by, sometimes even easier than legitimate copies.

Another black market area has been receipts. Romania's bureaucratic system makes the submission of receipts important in the claiming of expenses. Driving around certain areas of Bucharest, you may notice Roma people standing by the side of the road waving wads of paper at passing cars. These are bundles of receipts that they have printed to look like legitimately stamped documents. Employees buy them and use them to claim inflated expenses from their workplace. EU legislation on this kind of documentation looks set to reduce this scam.

THE LEGAL SYSTEM

Romania's legal system is modeled on the French Napoleonic Code. Trials are normally conducted in public, although there are exceptions in extenuating circumstances. In the past, Romania's courts resembled those in Charles Dickens's novel *Bleak House*. Cases could drag on almost indefinitely, with little hope of an equitable outcome. Despite EU-inspired improvements in recent years, the unpredictability of the legal system still deters potential investors.

The main problems are the same as beset other aspects of society: corruption and inefficiency. In the past, it was quite possible to bribe a judge. Cases could be adjourned or transferred for all manner of reasons. Many people with legitimate grievances would let them drop rather than face the probably futile challenge of trying to get redress through the courts. The country is now trying to do

something about this. Thanks to new
efforts and bodies to fight graft,
dozens of judges and lawyers
have been charged with
corruption. Still, many
companies continue to list
legal vagaries—the impossibility
of getting redress, the duration of trials, sudden
changes in the law without due process—as
being among the major obstacles to investing in
Romania. The EU has criticized the country for
its excessive use of the emergency ordinance
system, a Parliamentary measure intended to
speed up legislation in exceptional cases but
which was being used as a standard mechanism
to change the law.

BUSINESS HIERARCHIES

Traditionally, Romanian society is rigidly
hierarchical, with age, title, and position all highly
respected. Even today, wisdom, gained over time,
and seniority are the key factors in the decision-
making process, and the final say falls to the
highest-ranking person. Promotions, too, may be
awarded on length of service in the company,
rather than talent. This can be frustrating for
young, dynamic employees whose abilities go
unrecognized. The situation is most extreme in
state institutions and traditional firms.
Multinational corporations, or local firms run on
international principles, are now becoming more

common, and they are much more likely to reward individual talent and potential.

A similar difference can be observed in levels of formality. While in more modern or Western-style companies it is quite common for a new employee to use first names for everybody, up to and including the boss, in traditional Romanian companies people are sometimes expected to start by using a person's title and surname, or sometimes title and first name, until invited to use their first name only. The immediate use of first names would be presumptuous, although as usual there is some leeway for foreigners. Romanians may talk to subordinates in a curt way that sounds quite impolite to an outsider; equally, they will adopt a highly deferential tone to a superior.

INDEPENDENT THINKING

Given that until recent times independent thought was useless if not dangerous, it is little surprise that many people are far more comfortable following orders than using their initiative to solve problems. Another factor is the education system, which emphasizes rote learning at the expense of creativity. Some companies even fine their staff for mistakes—depleting a meager wage even further—so people's reluctance to depart from established ways of doing things is quite understandable. If your Romanian colleagues seem to be lacking in initiative, don't put this down to a lack of intelligence. It may be the working environment that punishes new ideas.

PASSING THE BUCK

The practice of fining employees for mistakes, rather than offering extra training or advice to correct the problem, leads in some parts to a culture of buck-passing. Few people are willing to assume responsibility for problems when doing so is likely to cost them financially. Also, with capitalism still quite new, employees may not have adequate knowledge of what their job should involve, and try to shift their responsibilities to someone else. The result is often one very overworked, conscientious person shouldering everyone else's duties.

RENEGOTIABILITY

The concept of negotiability in Romania is elastic. Whereas, usually, a price being negotiable means the seller may consider reducing it slightly, in Romania an agreed upon price could just as easily be subsequently negotiated upward by the seller, if he or she decides that the market value has risen, gets a better offer, or just feels like it. The fluctuating market, lack of business ethics, and still developing legal system are all factors in this "Wild East" mentality and behavior. When doing business, it is wise not to assume that any deal is done until all the contracts are signed— even then things can change, as we will see.

"YES" BECOMES "NO"

An irritating phenomenon for foreigners is the habit some Romanians have of entering into negotiations, taking them to an advanced stage, making an apparent agreement, and then pulling out at the last minute or simply disappearing. This can partly be explained by the Romanian propensity for telling people what they want to hear rather than the truth. The result is that instead of saying, "We've decided not to go ahead with the project," the person prefers to procrastinate and defer until it becomes obvious they have no intention of proceeding. This usually happens after protracted negotiations in which the other party started out highly enthusiastic to do business as soon as possible.

Another possible explanation is that Latin pride makes people reluctant to admit that they cannot afford the fee being asked for. Lower-ranked workers may not be granted much authority or allowed to use their own initiative, and decisions often have to be approved at different levels, so it could also be the case that a project one person proposes may be rejected by a higher-up. In any event, to avoid frustration, it is better not to assume things are definite until you have signed on the dotted line.

WOMEN IN BUSINESS

Despite the sexism rife in Romanian society, the business world offers something closer to parity. Communism encouraged women to seek employment—they still remained burdened with child-rearing and domestic duties—and they are well represented in the workforce, although few reach the higher echelons of business or politics. As elsewhere, the "female professions," such as teaching, nursing, and clerical work, are significantly worse paid than "male professions," such as construction, with women's wages typically around a fifth lower than men's. Although there is legislation that theoretically guarantees equal treatment at work, female employees and entrepreneurs still suffer from the widespread perception of a woman's chief value residing in her physical appearance and roles as wife and mother. As is common in Romania, nationality "trumps" gender, and a Western female expatriate is unlikely to experience much in the way of workplace sexism directly.

MEETINGS

As we shall see, many Romanian employees are remiss about returning phone calls and e-mails. While forward-thinking firms may be open to an e-mail approach, to be on the safe side, contact is probably best initiated by fax or letter. Confirm the meeting around two weeks in advance.

On the Day

Turn up on time. Romanians value punctuality, while not always adhering to it themselves—you may have to wait. If your counterparts do not speak English, take your own interpreter; this is something you can check in advance. Meetings tend to be formal, with business suits the expected attire. Shake hands firmly, meeting the other person's gaze.

Business cards are exchanged early on. The standard advice was to have the back of your card translated into Romanian, although this is no longer necessary, unless perhaps you are dealing with older provincial businesspeople. Include the date your company was founded if it has a long history, as stability can impress Romanians.

More traditional people may indicate where you should sit; younger ones will probably be more relaxed about this. Meetings tend to be warm, with drinks and snacks provided. This is not an invitation to relax totally, however; old-fashioned courtesy is the norm. Proceedings will probably be dominated by the most senior person present, who has the responsibility for all major decisions—save any concessions for this discussion. Romanians may negotiate toughly. Communicate directly, but sensitively, and do not use the hard sell. While there may be an agenda, this will not be adhered to rigidly. Interruption is a common element of conversation in Romania, but show respect to senior participants.

Presentations

Romanians are impressed by appearances; dressing your presentation up with laptops, the latest software, and other trappings is a good start. That said, it should still be thoroughly researched and with plenty of facts. Romanian audiences are likely to listen to your presentation politely, without interrupting, although it is advisable to keep it short and to the point.

CONTRACTS AND THEIR FULFILLMENT

Contracts, which may be subject to repeated revision, especially if circumstances change, must be registered with the relevant authority and therefore need to be in the local language. Certain offices are licensed to give official translations (*traduceri autorizate*), but be prepared for their proficiency in the foreign language to be low.

Once a contract is signed, maintain contact to check that things are progressing appropriately. Most Romanians respond best to clear leadership, rather than being left to figure things out on their own. Disputes tend to be settled out of court by lawyers, as neither party wants to enter the chronically understaffed legal system, which involves frequent delays and postponements. Legislation is not always business friendly, and while the country has been clamping down on corruption and political interference in the judiciary, these problems remain.

chapter nine

COMMUNICATING

DIRECTNESS

We have seen that Romanians are a straight-talking people whose directness can sometimes faze foreign visitors. A perfectly unemotional conversation can also sound so loud and brusque that it appears to be a heated argument. It is quite common for people, either within a family or in a work situation, to issue a series of orders to each other, none of which will be prefaced with the equivalent of "can you" or "would you mind." They argue, logically, that such phrases could imply that the other person has the right to refuse.

In social settings the majority of these orders will simply be ignored by Romanians as background noise, but a foreign visitor not aware of the phenomenon may be taken aback by a sudden series of directions on where to sit, what to eat, what to drink, and how to do it. In an office environment, the orders will be carried out without the subordinate feeling that he or she has been spoken to discourteously.

Ps and Qs

Because Romanians consider the essence of the message to be more important than how it is dressed up, conversation is punctuated with fewer polite phrases than you may be used to. Orders and requests will often be stated without a "please" (*vă rog* or *te rog*), and people may be served food and drink, at home or out, without feeling the need to thank the server. As with many similar customs, this is not intended as rudeness; it is possibly the outcome of an unfussy rural culture. Romanians are surprised by the number of "pleases" and "thank yous" that foreigners can fit into a short exchange, and many consider them quite unnecessary.

THE MISSING REPLY

The inefficient, distorted commerce that took place under Communism did not allow normal business etiquette to develop. This has many manifestations, but perhaps one of the most annoying for foreigners is people's tendency to ignore e-mails and phone calls. It is quite usual for employees, even in multinational companies, not to reply to important messages or to fail to phone back when they had promised to do so. This usually results in your having to chase them, in which case only a minority will apologize for their omission—the majority will not consider that they have done anything wrong. This is to some extent understandable if you are calling for a reason that benefits you (for example, to chase down payment), but wholly unfathomable when the person whose call, fax, or mail you are waiting for stands to benefit from replying (for example, when you are a customer).

MAIL

Step inside a Romanian post office and you could almost be back in the Communist era. They are uniformly dreary places, staffed by women on some of the lowest salaries in the country. When negotiating the frustratingly bureaucratic postal system, it is quite usual to be directed from one post office to another for the simple task of, say, sending a package by registered post. As well as dealing with mail, post offices are also where bills are paid. Occasionally long lines build up, and windows can be closed quite peremptorily.

Fortunately the service, once you can access it, is usually reliable, with airmail reaching Western Europe in around a week. In Bucharest, most larger post offices are open from 8:00 a.m. to 8:00 p.m. on Monday to Friday and from 8:00 a.m. to 2:00 p.m. on Saturday. Outside the capital, in more rural areas, weekday hours are usually from 9.30 a.m. to 5:00 p.m. Post offices have a red sign displaying the *Poşta Română* logo, a red background with a yellow "RO" on it and a horn in the colors of the Romanian flag.

TELEPHONES

The surge in popularity of cell phones has hit the national landline operator Romtelecom, as people abandon their landlines (known as fixed phones) to the detriment of its profits. It is also suffering from the competition in the landline sector that followed the market liberalization of 2003. Few young people rely on landlines outside their offices, even though calls from one landline to another remain the cheapest way to communicate.

CELL PHONES

Cell phones have caught on in a big way in Romania. The National Authority for the Regulation of Communications reported that at the start of 2007, the local cell phone penetration rate was 80 percent, up from 69 percent just six months earlier. The figure is still rising rapidly. Virtually every young person has a cell phone—often two or three. Even older people are starting to use the technology, typically encouraged by their children. The main two providers are Vodafone (previously called Connex) and Orange. Some way behind the front two are Zapp, which targets corporate clients, Cosmote, which has quickly built up a client base through some very cheap tariffs, and Telefonica, which targets users in rural areas. Richer customers tend to have contracts, which they pay for with a monthly bill, while the less well-off, including a lot of students, have prepay deals, where they pay to put credit on their phones in advance. Text messages are very popular as a way to keep in touch and make arrangements.

One interesting phenomenon is "the beep." People who have less money will call the person they wish to speak to, hanging up before the phone can be answered. That person is expected to phone them back, and so foot the cost of the call. While some people consider the beep rather cheap and cheeky, others see it as a way of allowing poorer people—particularly those on prepay deals where the cost of calls is high—to stay in touch, and if you accidentally answer a call that was meant to be a beep, you may be greeted by a rather disgruntled caller.

There are few social restrictions on where a cell phone can be used. Drivers routinely talk on the phone while behind the wheel, even though this is illegal. Few people would consider it bad manners to make or receive a call while eating in a restaurant. Mobile phones frequently ring in the cinema, and while some people will go outside to answer the call, many will conduct their conversation in the auditorium during the film. Although it is rarer, the same can happen at a live event such as a classical music concert.

THE INTERNET

Despite their low incomes and the late start that many technological developments have had in

Romania, people have eagerly embraced the Internet, both for work and particularly for leisure. Romanians are keen chat room participants, and most people—young people at least—have e-mail, with Yahoo! being the most popular provider. Many employees have Yahoo! Messenger open at work for much of the day—often to the chagrin of their bosses.

Until recently, few people were able to afford a computer at home. Increasing wages and government programs to facilitate computer ownership among poor families have changed this, with many city dwellers and even some rural households now owning a PC or laptop. Internet connection is usually through one of the two main cable TV firms, Astral and RCS/RDS. Prices are high compared to Western Europe, and connection speeds are typically lower. Many Romanians prefer to access the Internet through a neighborhood network, which involves wires going from one apartment to another. This gives faster speeds for file sharing and Romanian Web sites (which end in .ro), but is slower for international domains.

THE MEDIA

From its propaganda-fueled days under Communism, the media is now becoming more professional and fit for purpose. Although it is rapidly improving with help from organizations such as the active and professional Center for

Independent Journalism, a project of the Independent Journalism Foundation in New York, all forms of media continue to suffer from controlling interests and poor quality. The ideal of a powerful press that holds the guilty to account is still a long way off. A current concern is that a few owners, mostly businessmen of dubious repute, are gaining control over multiple media outlets.

We have seen that television is the main medium in terms of influence, share of advertising (around 90 percent), and takeup. The state-run service is TVR, or *Televiziunea Română*, which is funded by a license fee as well as advertising sales. Its freedom from government interference is questionable, and the station was accused of favoring the incumbent Social Democrats in the 2004 election. The top two private stations, Pro TV and Antena 1, attract higher audiences. There is no national channel in English, but because most people have cable there are plenty of international options, and much local output consists of American imports. News programs tend to focus on car accidents and salacious gossip rather than hard news.

The written media represents a smaller portion of the market. It is overwhelmingly tabloid, with the market leader a lowbrow, sensationalist, and often inaccurate daily called *Libertatea*. Some titles do aim higher—business title *Ziarul*

Financiar is the only quality paper, and *Adevărul*, *Quotidien*, *Evenimentul Zilei*, *Curentul*, and *Jurnalul National* are somewhere between tabloid and quality. Romania does not currently offer the standard of written journalism you would find in the West. Part of the reason for this is that many newspapers are run not for their own sake but as propaganda tools of the owners. Publications, TV, and radio stations tend to be concentrated in the hands of a few media magnates, who use them to promote and further their other business interests. There are a few honorable exceptions, such as the satirical *Academia Cațavencu*, which seldom shies away from criticizing the powerful and had a huge portion of its print run allegedly bought up by the Social Democrats when it printed a supplement parodying the party in the run-up to the 2004 elections. Even that title is now owned by a controversial businessman said by some to have been involved in a pyramid selling scheme.

The English-language press is concentrated in the capital. The main titles are *Nine O'Clock*, a poorly written daily; *Business Review*, an informative weekly containing a range of business, political, and cultural coverage; *Bucharest In Your Pocket*, an entertaining and honest bimonthly listings guide to the city; *Vivid*, a glossy magazine with features from mostly international writers; and *Expat Life*, a lowbrow satirical monthly aimed mostly at male, middle-aged expatriates.

CONCLUSION

If you have made it this far undeterred by what
you have read, you are probably the kind of
visitor who could get a lot out of traveling in
Romania. It's not the easiest place to spend time,
but the rewards by far outweigh the irritations.

The aim of this book is not only to prepare you
for some of the frustrations you might face, but
also to set out the liberating, exciting, and
heartwarming aspects of Romanian life. In a fast-
developing country, tangible changes are visible
even in a short stay, buoyed by the people's hope
that this time things may be better.

Despite the many setbacks and deprivations
they have suffered, the Romanians remain warm
and welcoming, and not even grinding poverty
can stop them from being the most generous
hosts. Guests in Romania are never regarded as a
nuisance, and as a guest in their homeland you
have privileged status; people will go out of their
way to help you, seldom with any motive other
than to help a stranger in a foreign land and create
a good impression of their country. This is just
one of the national characteristics that will put all
the Communist hangovers in perspective.
Romania's faults are well documented; its many
endearments still await discovery.

Further Reading

Deletant, Dennis. *Romania Under Communist Rule*. London: Center for Romanian Studies, 1999.

Gallagher, Tom. *Modern Romania: The End of Communism, the Failure of Democratic Reform, and the Theft of a Nation*. New York: New York University Press, 2005.

Klepper, Nicolae. *Taste of Romania: Its Cookery and Glimpses of Its History, Folklore, Art, Literature, and Poetry*. New York: Hippocrene Books, expanded edition 1999.

Mandache, Diana. *Later Chapters of My Life: The Lost Memoir of Queen Marie of Romania*. Gloucestershire, UK: Sutton Publishing, 2004.

Manea, Norman. *The Hooligan's Return: A Memoir*. New York: Farrar, Straus and Giroux, 2003.

Pacepa, Ion Mihai. *Red Horizons: The True Story of Nicolae and Elena Ceausescu's Crimes, Lifestyle, and Corruption*. Washington, D.C.: Regnery Publishing, Inc., 1990.

Siani-Davies, Peter. *The Romanian Revolution of December 1989*. New York: Cornell University Press, 2005.

Voiculescu, Razvan. *Romania: The Humble Port of Splendor*. Bucharest: Humanitas, 2005.

Index

Acknowledgments

This book is dedicated to my dad, who fuelled my appetite for foreign travel.

I would like to thank Vasile Szakacs and Simona Fodor for their invaluable help with the manuscript.